FROM CANAL BOY
TO PRESIDENT

Cover art: Maya Rae Miller

From Canal Boy to President: The Boyhood and Manhood of James A. Garfield

All new material copyright © 2018 Jon S. Miller.

All inquiries should be addressed to the editor, Jon Miller
(mjon@uakron.edu)

ISBN 978-1-629221-15-1

FROM CANAL BOY TO PRESIDENT

THE BOYHOOD AND MANHOOD OF JAMES A. GARFIELD

Horatio Alger, Jr.
Ed. Jon Miller

The University of Akron
Akron, Ohio

TO
HARRY AND JAMES GARFIELD
WHOSE PRIVATE SORROW
IS THE PUBLIC GRIEF,
THIS MEMORIAL
OF THEIR ILLUSTRIOUS FATHER
IS INSCRIBED
WITH THE WARMEST SYMPATHY.

A NOTE ON THE TEXT.

This edition of Horatio Alger, Jr.'s biography of James Garfield was prepared by Jon Miller for the use of the students at The University of Akron.

The text follows the 1881 John R. Anderson & Company edition, with some updates to the formatting of quoted material. New running heads and an appendix have also been added.

PREFACE.

If I am asked why I add one to the numerous Lives of our dead President, I answer, in the words of Hon. Chauncey M. Depew, because "our annals afford no such incentive to youth as does his life, and it will become one of the Republic's household stories."

I have conceived, therefore, that a biography, written with a view to interest young people in the facts of his great career, would be a praiseworthy undertaking. The biography of General Garfield, however imperfectly executed, can not but be profitable to the reader. In this story, which I have made as attractive as I am able, I make no claim to originality. I have made free use of such materials as came within my reach, including incidents and reminiscences made public during the last summer, and I trust I have succeeded, in a measure, in conveying a correct idea of a character whose nobility we have only learned to appreciate since death has snatched our leader from us.

I take pleasure in acknowledging my obligations to two Lives of Garfield, one by Edmund Kirke, the other by Major J.M. Bundy. Such of my readers as desire a more extended account of the later life of Gen. Garfield, I refer to these well-written and instructive works.

HORATIO ALGER, JR.
New York, Oct. 8, 1881.

CONTENTS.

CHAPTER I.
THE FIRST PAIR OF SHOES.

From a small and rudely-built log-cabin a sturdy boy of four years issued, and looked earnestly across the clearing to the pathway that led through the surrounding forest. His bare feet pressed the soft grass, which spread like a carpet before the door.

"What are you looking for, Jimmy?" asked his mother from within the humble dwelling.

"I'm looking for Thomas," said Jimmy.

"It's hardly time for him yet. He won't be through work till after sunset."

"Then I wish the sun would set quick," said Jimmy.

"That is something we can not hasten, my son. God makes the sun to rise and to set in its due season."

This idea was probably too advanced for Jimmy's comprehension, for he was but four years of age, and the youngest of a family of four children. His father had died two years before, leaving a young widow, and four children, the eldest but nine, in sore straits. A long and severe winter lay before the little family, and they had but little corn garnered to carry them through till the next harvest. But the young widow was a brave woman and a devoted mother.

"God will provide for us," she said, but sometimes it seemed a mystery how that provision was to come. More than once, when the corn was low in the bin, she went to bed without her own supper, that her four children, who were blessed with hearty appetites, might be satisfied. But when twelve months had gone by, and the new harvest came in, the fields which she and her oldest boy had planted yielded enough to place them beyond the fear of want. God did help them, but it was because they helped themselves.

But beyond the barest necessaries the little family neither expected nor obtained much. Clothing cost money, and there was very little money in the log-cabin, or indeed in the whole settlement, if settlement it can be called. There was no house within a mile, and the village a mile and a half away contained only a school-house, a grist-mill, and a little log store and dwelling.

Two weeks before my story opens, a farmer living not far away called at the log-cabin. Thomas, the oldest boy, was at work in a field near the house.

"Do you want to see mother?" he asked.

"No, I want to see you."

"All right, sir! Here I am," said Thomas, smiling pleasantly.

"How old are you?" asked the farmer.

"Eleven years old, sir."

The farmer surveyed approvingly the sturdy frame, broad shoulders, and muscular arms of the boy, and said, after a pause, "You look pretty strong of your age."

"Oh, yes, sir," answered Thomas, complacently "I am strong."

"And you are used to farm work?"

"Yes, sir. I do about all the outdoor work at home, being the only boy. Of course, there is Jimmy, but he is only four, and that's too young to work on the farm."

"What does he want?" thought Thomas.

He soon learned.

"I need help on my farm, and I guess you will suit me," said Mr. Conrad, though that was not his name. In fact, I don't know his name, but that will do as well as any other.

"I don't know whether mother can spare me, but I can ask her," said Thomas. "What are you willing to pay?"

"I'll give you twelve dollars a month, but you'll have to make long days."

Twelve dollars a month! Tom's eyes sparkled with joy, for to him it seemed an immense sum— and it would go very far in the little family.

"I am quite sure mother will let me go," he said. "I'll go in and ask her."

"Do so, sonny, and I'll wait for you here."

Thomas swung open the plank door, and entered the cabin.

It was about twenty feet one way by thirty the other. It had three small windows, a deal floor, and the spaces between the logs of which it was built were filled in with clay. It was certainly an humble dwelling, and the chances are that not one of my young readers is so poor as not to afford a better. Yet, it was not uncomfortable. It afforded fair protection from the heat of summer, and the cold of winter, and was after all far more desirable as a home than the crowded tenements of our larger cities, for those who occupied it had but to open the door and windows to breathe the pure air of heaven, uncontaminated by foul odors or the taint of miasma.

"Mother," said Thomas, "Mr. Conrad wants to hire me to work on his farm, and he is willing to pay me twelve dollars a month. May I go?"

"Ask Mr. Conrad to come in, Thomas."

The farmer entered, and repeated his request.

Mrs. Garfield, for this was the widow's name, was but little over thirty. She had a strong, thoughtful face, and a firm mouth, that spoke a decided character. She was just the woman to grapple with adversity, and turning her unwearied hands to any work, to rear up her children in the fear of the Lord, and provide for their necessities as well as circumstances would admit.

She didn't like to spare Thomas, for much of his work would be thrown upon her, but there was great lack of ready money and the twelve dollars were a powerful temptation.

"I need Thomas at home," she said slowly, "but I need the money more. He may go, if he likes."

"I will go," said Thomas promptly.

"How often can you let him come home?" was the next question.

"Every fortnight, on Saturday night. He shall bring his wages then."

This was satisfactory, and Thomas, not stopping to change his clothes, for he had but one suit, went off with his employer.

His absence naturally increased his mother's work, and was felt as a sore loss by Jimmy, who was in the habit of following him about, and watching him when he was at work. Sometimes his brother gave the little fellow a trifle to do, and Jimmy was always pleased to help, for he was fond of work, and when he grew older and stronger he was himself a sturdy and indefatigable worker in ways not dreamed of then.

The first fortnight was up, and Thomas was expected home. No one was more anxious to see him than his little brother, and that was why Jimmy had come out from his humble home, and was looking so earnestly across the clearing.

At last he saw him, and ran as fast as short legs could carry him to meet his brother.

"Oh, Tommy, how I've missed you!" he said.

"Have you, Jimmy?" asked Thomas, passing his arm around his little brother's neck. "I have missed you too, and all the family. Are all well?"

"Oh, yes."

"That is good."

As they neared the cabin Mrs. Garfield came out, and welcomed her oldest boy home.

"We are all glad to see you, Thomas," she said. "How have you got along?"

"Very well, mother."

"Was the work hard?"

"The hours were pretty long. I had to work fourteen hours a day."

"That is too long for a boy of your age to work," said his mother anxiously.

"Oh, it hasn't hurt me, mother," said Thomas, laughing. "Besides, you must remember I have been well paid. What do you say to that?"

He drew from his pocket twelve silver

half-dollars, and laid them on the table, a glittering heap.

"Is it all yours, Tommy?" asked his little brother wonderingly.

"No, it belongs to mother. I give it to her."

"Thank you, Thomas," said Mrs. Garfield, "but at least you ought to be consulted about how it shall be spent. Is there anything you need for yourself?"

"Oh, never mind me! I want Jimmy to have a pair of shoes."

Jimmy looked with interest at his little bare feet, and thought he would like some shoes. In fact they would be his first, for thus far in life he had been a barefooted boy.

"Jimmy shall have his shoes," said Mrs. Garfield; "when you see the shoemaker ask him to come here as soon as he can make it convenient."

So, a few days later the shoemaker, who may possibly have had no shop of his own, called at the log-cabin, measured Jimmy for a pair of shoes, and made them on the spot, boarding out a part of his pay.

The first pair of shoes made an important epoch in Jimmy Garfield's life, for it was decided that he could now go to school.

CHAPTER II.
GROWING IN WISDOM AND STATURE.

The school was in the village a mile and a half away. It was a long walk for a little boy of four, but sometimes his sister Mehetabel, now thirteen years old, carried him on her back. When in winter the snow lay deep on the ground Jimmy's books were brought home, and he recited his lessons to his mother.

This may be a good time to say something of the family whose name in after years was to become a household word throughout the republic. They had been long in the country. They were literally one of the first families, for in 1636, only sixteen years after the Pilgrims landed on Plymouth rock, and the same year that Harvard College was founded, Edward Garfield, who had come from the edge of Wales, settled in Watertown, Massachusetts, less than four miles from the infant college, and there for more than a century was the family home, as several moss-grown headstones in the ancient graveyard still testify.

They did their part in the Revolutionary war, and it was not till the war was over that Solomon Garfield, the great grandfather of the future President, removed to the town of Worcester, Otsego County, N.Y. Here lived the Garfields for two generations. Then Abram Garfield, the father of James, moved to Northeastern Ohio, and bought a tract of eighty acres, on which stood the log-cabin, built by himself, in which our story opens. His wife belonged to a distinguished family of New England—the Ballous—and possessed the strong traits of her kindred.

But the little farm of eighty acres was smaller now. Abram Garfield died in debt, and his wife sold off fifty acres to pay his creditors, leaving thirty, which with her own industry and that of her oldest son served to maintain her little family.

The school-house was so far away that Mrs. Garfield, who appreciated the importance of education for her children, offered her neighbors a site for a new school-house on her own land, and one was built. Here winter after winter came teachers, some of limited qualifications, to instruct the children of the neighborhood, and here Jimmy enlarged his stock of book-learning by slow degrees.

The years passed, and still they lived in the humble log-cabin, till at the age of twenty-one Thomas came home from Michigan, where he had been engaged in clearing land for a farmer, bringing seventy-five dollars in gold.

"Now, mother," he said, "you shall have a framed house."

Seventy-five dollars would not pay for a framed house, but he cut timber himself, got out the boards, and added his own labor, and that of Jimmy, now fourteen years old, and so the house was built, and the log-cabin became a thing of the past. But it had been their home for a long time, and doubtless many happy days had been spent beneath its humble roof.

While the house was being built, Jimmy learned one thing—that he was handy with tools, and was well fitted to become a carpenter. When the joiner told him that he was born to be a carpenter, he thought with joy that this unexpected talent would enable him to help his mother, and earn something toward the family expenses. So, for the next two years he worked at this new business when opportunity offered, and if my reader should go to Chagrin Falls, Ohio, he could probably find upon inquiry several barns in the vicinity which Jimmy helped to build.

He still went to school, however, and obtained such knowledge of the mysteries of grammar, arithmetic, and geography as could be obtained in the common schools of that day.

But Jimmy Garfield was not born to be a carpenter, and I believe never got so far along as to assist in building a house.

He was employed to build a wood-shed for a black-salter, ten miles away from his mother's house, and when the job was finished his employer fell into conversation with him, and being a man of limited acquirements himself, was impressed by the boy's surprising stock of knowledge.

"You kin read, you kin write, and you are death on figgers," he said to him one day. "If you'll stay with me, keep my 'counts, and 'tend to the saltery, I'll find you, and give you fourteen dollars a month."

Jimmy was dazzled by this brilliant offer. He felt that to accept it would be to enter upon the high-road to riches, and he resolved to do so if his mother would consent. Ten miles he trudged through the woods to ask his mother's consent, which with some difficulty he obtained, for she did not know to what influences he might be subjected, and so he got started in a new business.

Whether he would have fulfilled his employer's prediction, and some day been at the head of a saltery of his own, we can not tell; but in time he became dissatisfied with his situation, and returning home, waited for Providence to indicate some new path on which to enter.

One thing, however, was certain: he would not be content to remain long without employment. He had an active temperament, and would have been happiest when busy, even if he had not known that his mother needed the fruits of his labor.

He had one source of enjoyment while employed by the black-salter, which he fully appreciated. Strange to say, his employer had a library, that is, he had a small collection of books, gathered by his daughter, prominent among which were Marryatt's novels, and "Sinbad the Sailor." They opened a new world to his young accountant, and gave him an intense desire to see the world, and especially to cross the great sea, even in the capacity of a sailor. At home there was no library, not from the lack of literary taste, but because there was no money to spend for anything but necessaries.

He had not been long at home when a neighbor, entering one day, said, "James, do you want a job?"

"Yes," answered James, eagerly.

"There's a farmer in Newburg wants some wood chopped."

"I can do it," said James, quietly.

"Then you'd better go and see him."

Newburg is within the present limits of Cleveland, and thither James betook himself the next day.

He was a stout boy, with the broad shoulders

and sturdy frame of his former ancestors, and he was sure he could give satisfaction.

The farmer, dressed in homespun, looked up as the boy approached.

"Are you Mr. ——?" asked James.

"Yes."

"I heard that you wanted some wood chopped."

"Yes, but I am not sure if you can do it," answered the farmer, surveying the boy critically.

"I can do it," said James, confidently.

"Very well, you can try. I'll give you seven dollars for the job."

The price was probably satisfactory, for James engaged to do the work. There proved to be twenty-five cords, and no one, I think, will consider that he was overpaid for his labor.

He was fortunate, at least, in the scene of his labor, for it was on the shore of Lake Erie, and as he lifted his eyes from his work they rested on the broad bosom of the beautiful lake, almost broad enough as it appeared to be the ocean itself, which he had a strange desire to traverse in search of the unknown lands of which he had read or dreamed.

I suppose there are few boys who have not at some time fancied that they should like "a life on the ocean wave, and a home on the rolling deep." I have in mind a friend, now a physician, who at the age of fifteen left a luxurious home, with the reluctant permission of his parents, for a voyage before the mast to Liverpool, beguiled by one of the fascinating narratives of Herman Melville. But the romance very soon wore off, and by the time the boy reached Halifax, where the ship put in, he was so seasick, and so sick of the sea, that he begged to be left on shore to return home as he might. The captain had received secret instructions from the parents to accede to such a wish, and the boy was landed, and in due time returned home as a passenger. So it is said that George Washington had an early passion for the sea, and would have become a sailor but for the pain he knew it would give his mother.

James kept his longings to himself for the present, and returned home with the seven dollars he had so hardly earned.

There was more work for him to do. A Mr. Treat wanted help during the haying and harvesting season, and offered employment to the boy, who was already strong enough to do almost as much as a man; for James already had a good reputation as a faithful worker. "Whatever his hands found to do, he did it with his might," and he was by no means fastidious as to the kind of work, provided it was honest and honorable.

When the harvest work was over James made known his passion for the sea.

Going to his mother, he said: "Mother, I want above all things to go to sea."

"Go to sea!" replied his mother in dismay. "What has put such an idea into your head?"

"It has been in my head for a long time," answered the boy quietly. "I have thought of nothing else for the last year."

CHAPTER III.
IN QUEST OF FORTUNE.

James had so persuaded himself that the sea was his vocation, and was so convinced of the pleasures and advantages it would bring, that it had not occurred to him that his mother would object.

"What made you think of the sea, James?" his mother asked with a troubled face.

"It was the books I read last year, at the black salter's. Oh, mother, did you ever read Marryatt's novels, and *Sinbad the Sailor*?"

"I have read *Sinbad the Sailor*, but you know that is a fairy story, my son."

"It may be, but Marryatt's stories are not. It must be splendid to travel across the mighty ocean, and see foreign countries."

"A sailor doesn't have the chance to see much. You have no idea of the hardships of his life."

"I am used to hardships, and I am not afraid of hard work. But you seem disappointed, mother. What have you thought of for me?"

"I have hoped, James, that you might become a learned man, perhaps a college professor. Surely that would be better than to be a common sailor."

"But I wouldn't stay a common sailor, mother. I would be a captain some time."

I suppose there is no doubt that, had James followed the sea, he would have risen to the command of a ship, but the idea did not seem to dazzle his mother.

"If you go to sea I shall lose you," said his mother. "A sailor can spend very little time with his family. Think carefully, my son. I believe your present fancy will be short-lived, and you will some day wonder that you ever entertained it."

Such, however, was not the boy's idea at the time. His mother might have reason on her side, but it takes more than reason to dissipate a boy's passion for the sea.

"You speak of my becoming a scholar, mother," he said, "but there doesn't seem much chance of it. I see nothing but work as a carpenter, or on the farm."

"You don't know what God may have in store for you, my son. As you say, there seems no way open at present for you to become a scholar; but if you entertain the desire the way will be open. Success comes to him who is in earnest."

"What, then, do you want me to do, mother! Do you wish me to stay at home?"

"No, for there seems little for you to do here. Go to Cleveland, if you like, and seek some respectable employment. If, after a time, you find your longing for the sea unconquered, it will be time to look out for a berth on board ship."

James, in spite of his earnest longing to go to sea, was a reasonable boy, and he did not object to his mother's plan. The next morning he tied his slender stock of clothing in a small bundle, bade a tearful good-bye to his mother, whose loving glances followed him far along his road, and with hope and enthusiasm trudged over a hard road to Cleveland, that beautiful city, whither, nearly forty years afterward, he was to be carried in funereal state, amid the tears of countless thousands. In that city where his active life began, it was to finish.

A long walk was before him, for Cleveland was seventeen miles away. He stopped to rest at intervals, and it was not until the sun had set and darkness enveloped the town that he entered it with weary feet.

He betook himself to a cheap boarding-place whither he had been directed, and soon retired to bed. His fatigue brought him a good night's sleep, and he woke refreshed and cheered to look about him and decide upon his future plans.

Cleveland does not compare in size with New York, Philadelphia, or Boston, and thirty-five years ago it was much smaller than now. But compared with James' native place, and the villages near him, it was an impressive place. There were large business blocks, and handsome churches, and paved streets, and a general city-like appearance which interested James greatly. On the whole, even if he had to give up going to sea, he thought he might enjoy himself in such a lively place as this. But of course he must find employment.

So he went into a store and inquired if they wanted a boy.

"What can you do?" asked the storekeeper, looking at the boy with his countrified air and rustic suit.

"I can read, write, and cipher," answered James.

"Indeed!" said the storekeeper smiling. "All our boys can do that. Is that all you can do?"

James might have answered that he could chop wood, work at carpentering, plant and harvest, but he knew very well that these accomplishments would be but little service to him here. Indeed, he was rather puzzled to know what he could do that would earn him a living in a smart town like Cleveland. However, he didn't much expect to find his first application successful, so he entered another store and preferred his request.

"You won't suit us," was the brusque reply. "You come from the country, don't you?"

"Yes, sir."

"You look like it. Well, I will give you a piece of advice."

"What is that, sir?"

"Go back there. You are better suited to country than the city. I daresay you would make a very good hand on a farm. We need different sort of boys here."

This was discouraging. James didn't know why he would not do for a city store or office. He was strong enough, and he thought he knew enough, for he had not at present much idea of what was taught at seminaries of a higher grade than the district schools he had been accustomed to attend.

"Well," he said to himself, "I've done what mother asked me to do. I've tried to get a place here, and there doesn't seem to be a place for me. After all, I don't know but I'd better go to sea."

Cleveland was not of course a sea-port, but

it had considerable lake trade, and had a line of piers.

James found his way to the wharves, and his eye lighted up as he saw the sloops and schooners which were engaged in inland trade. He had never seen a real ship, or those schooners and sloops would have had less attraction for him.

In particular his attention was drawn to one schooner, not over-clean or attractive, but with a sea-faring look, as if it had been storm-tossed and buffeted. Half a dozen sailors were on board, but they were grimed and dirty, and looked like habitual drinkers—probably James would not have fancied becoming like one of these, but he gave little thought to their appearance. He only thought how delightful it would be to have such a floating home.

"Is the captain on board?" the boy ventured to ask.

"He's down below," growled the sailor whom he addressed.

"Will he soon come up?"

He was answered in the affirmative.

So James lingered until the man he inquired for came up.

He was a brutal-looking man, as common in appearance as any of the sailors whom he commanded, and the boy was amazed at his bearing. Surely that man was not his ideal of a ship-captain. He thought of him as a sort of prince, but there was nothing princely about the miserable, bloated wretch before him.

Still he preferred his application.

"Do you want a new hand?" asked James.

His answer was a volley of oaths and curses that made James turn pale, for he had never uttered an oath in his life, and had never listened to anything so disgusting as the tirade to which he was forced to listen.

He sensibly concluded that nothing was to be gained by continuing the conversation with such a man. He left the schooner's deck with a feeling of discomfiture. He had never suspected that sailors talked or acted like the men he saw.

Still he clung to the idea that all sailors were not like this captain. Perhaps again the rebuff he received was in consequence of his rustic appearance. The captain might be prejudiced against him, just as the shop-keepers had been, though the latter certainly had not expressed themselves in such rude and profane language. He might not be fit for a sailor yet, but he could prepare himself.

He bethought himself of a cousin of his, by name Amos Letcher, who had not indeed arrived at the exalted position of captain of a schooner, but was content with the humbler position of captain of a canal-boat on the Ohio and Pennsylvania Canal.

This seemed to James a lucky thought.

"I will go to Amos Letcher," he said to himself. "Perhaps he can find me a situation on a canal-boat, and that will be the next thing to being on board a ship."

This thought put fresh courage into the boy, and he straightway inquired for the *Evening*

Star, which was the name of the boat commanded by his cousin.

CHAPTER IV.
ON THE TOW-PATH.

Captain Letcher regarded his young cousin in surprise.

"Well, Jimmy, what brings you to Cleveland?" he asked.

"I came here to ship on the lake," the boy answered. "I tried first to get a place in a store, as I promised mother, but I found no opening. I would rather be a sailor."

"I am afraid your choice is not a good one; a good place on land is much better than going to sea. Have you tried to get a berth?"

"Yes, I applied to the captain of a schooner, but he swore at me and called me a land-lubber."

"So you are," returned his cousin smiling "Well, what are your plans now?"

"Can't you give me a place?"

"What, on the canal?"

"Yes cousin."

"I suppose you think that would be the next thing to going to sea?"

"It might prepare me for it."

"Well," said Captain Letcher, good-naturedly, "I will see what I can do for you. Can you drive a pair of horses?"

"Oh, yes."

"Then I will engage you. The pay is not very large, but you will live on the boat."

"How much do you pay?" asked James, who

was naturally interested in the answer to this question.

"We pay from eight to ten dollars a month, according to length of service and fidelity. Of course, as a new hand, you can not expect ten dollars."

"I shall be satisfied with eight, cousin."

"Now, as to your duties. You will work six hours on and six hours off. That's what we call a trick—the six hours on, I mean. So you will have every other six hours to rest, or do anything you like; that is, after you have attended to the horses."

"Horses!" repeated James, puzzled; for the animals attached to the boat at that moment were mules.

"Some of our horses are mules," said Captain Letcher, smiling. "However, it makes no difference. You will have to feed and rub them down, and then you can lie down in your bunk, or do anything else you like."

"That won't be very hard work," said James, cheerfully.

"Oh, I forgot to say that you can ride or walk, as you choose. You can rest yourself by changing from one to the other."

James thought he should like to ride on horseback, as most boys do. It was not, however, so good fun as he anticipated. A canal-boat horse is by no means a fiery or spirited creature. His usual gait is from two to two and a half miles an hour, and to a boy of quick, active temperament the slowness must be rather exasperating. Yet, in the course of a day a boat went a considerable distance. It usually made fifty, and sometimes sixty miles a day. The rate depended on the number of locks it had to pass through.

Probably most of my young readers understand the nature of a lock. As all water seeks a level, there would be danger in an uneven country that some parts of the canal would be left entirely dry, and in others the water would overflow. For this reason at intervals locks are constructed, composed of brief sections of the canal barricaded at each end by gates. When a boat is going down, the near gates are thrown open and the boat enters the lock, the water rushing in till a level is secured; then the upper gates are closed, fastening the boat in the lock. Next the lower gates are opened, the water in the lock seeks the lower level of the other section of the canal, and the boat moves out of the lock, the water subsiding gradually beneath it. Next, the lower gates are closed, and the boat proceeds on its way. It will easily be understood, when the case is reversed, and the boat is going up, how after being admitted into the lock it will be lifted up to the higher level when the upper gates are thrown open.

If any of my young readers find it difficult to understand my explanation, I advise them to read Jacob Abbot's excellent book, *Rollo on the Erie Canal*, where the whole matter is lucidly explained.

Railroads were not at that time as common as now, and the canal was of much more importance and value as a means of conveying freight. Sometimes passengers traveled that way, when they were in not much of a hurry, but there were no express canal-boats, and a man who chose to travel in that way must have abundant leisure on his hands. There is some difference between traveling from two to two and a half miles an hour, and between thirty and forty, as most of our railroad express trains do.

James did not have to wait long after his engagement before he was put on duty. With boyish pride he mounted one of the mules and led the other. A line connected the mules with the boat, which was drawn slowly and steadily through the water. James felt the responsibility of his situation. It was like going to sea on a small scale, though the sea was but a canal. At all events, he felt that he had more important work to do than if he were employed as a boy on one of the lake schooners.

James was at this time fifteen; a strong, sturdy boy, with a mass of auburn hair, partly covered by a loose-fitting hat. He had a bright, intelligent face, and an earnest look that attracted general attention. Yet, to one who saw the boy guiding the patient mule along the tow-path, it would have seemed a most improbable prediction, that one day the same hand would guide the ship of State, a vessel of much more consequence than the humble canal-boat.

There was one comfort, at any rate. Though in his rustic garb he was not well enough dressed to act as clerk in a Cleveland store, no one complained that he was not well enough attired for a canal-boy.

It will occur to my young reader that, though the work was rather monotonous, there was not much difficulty or danger connected with it. But even the guidance of a canal-boat has its perplexities, and James was not long in his new position before he realized it.

It often happened that a canal-boat going up encountered another going down, and *vice versa.* Then care has to be exercised by the respective drivers lest their lines get entangled.

All had been going on smoothly till James saw another boat coming. It might have been his inexperience, or it might have been the carelessness of the other driver, but at any rate the lines got entangled. Meanwhile the boat, under the impetus that had been given it, kept on its way until it was even with the horses, and seemed likely to tow them along.

"Whip up your team, Jim, or your line will ketch on the bridge!" called out the steersman.

The bridge was built over a waste-way which occurred just ahead, and it was necessary for James to drive over it.

The caution was heeded, but too late. James whipped up his mules, but when he had reached the middle of the bridge the rope tightened, and before the young driver fairly understood what awaited him, he and his team were jerked into the canal. Of course he was thrown off the animal he was riding, and found himself struggling in the water side by side with the astonished mules. The situation was a ludicrous one, but it was also attended with some danger. Even if he did not drown, and the canal was probably deep enough for that, he stood in some danger of being kicked by the terrified mules.

The boy, however, preserved his presence of mind, and managed, with help, to get out himself and to get his team out.

Then Captain Letcher asked him, jocosely, "What were you doing in the canal, Jim?"

"I was just taking my morning bath," answered the boy, in the same vein.

"You'll do," said the captain, struck by the boy's coolness.

Six hours passed, and James' "trick" was over. He and his mules were both relieved from duty. Both were allowed to come on board the boat and rest for a like period, while the other driver took his place on the tow-path.

"Well, Jim, how do you like it as far as you've got?" asked the captain.

"I like it," answered the boy.

"Shall you be ready to take another bath to-morrow morning?" asked his cousin, slyly.

"I think one bath a week will be sufficient," was the answer.

Feeling a natural interest in his young cousin, Amos Letcher thought he would examine him a little, to see how far his education had advanced. Respecting his own ability as an examiner he had little doubt, for he had filled the proud position of teacher in Steuben County, Indiana, for three successive winters.

"I suppose you have been to school more or less, Jim?" he said.

"Oh, yes," answered the boy.

"What have you studied?"

James enumerated the ordinary school branches. They were not many, for his acquirements were not extensive; but he had worked well, and was pretty well grounded as far as he had gone.

CHAPTER V.
AN IMPORTANT CONVERSATION.

"I've taught school myself," said Captain Letcher, complacently. "I taught for three winters in Indiana."

James, who, even then, had a high opinion of learning, regarded the canal-boat captain with increased respect.

"I didn't know that," he answered, duly impressed.

"Yes, I've had experience as a teacher. Now, if you don't mind, I'll ask you a few questions, and find out how much you know. We've got plenty of time, for it's a long way to Pancake Lock."

"Don't ask me too hard questions," said the boy. "I'll answer the best I know."

Upon this Captain Letcher, taking a little time to think, began to question his young cousin in the different branches he had enumerated. The questions were not very hard, for the good captain, though he had taught school in Indiana, was not a profound scholar.

James answered every question promptly and accurately, to the increasing surprise of his employer.

The latter paused.

"Haven't you any more questions?" asked James.

"No, I don't think of any."

"Then may I ask you some?"

"Yes, if you want to," answered the captain, rather surprised.

"Very well," said James. "A man went to a shoemaker and bought a pair of boots, for which he was to pay five dollars. He offered a fifty-dollar bill, which the shoemaker sent out and had changed. He paid his customer forty-five dollars in change, and the latter walked off with the boots. An hour later he ascertained that the bill was a counterfeit, and he was obliged to pay back fifty dollars in good money to the man who had changed the bill for him. Now, how much did he lose?"

"That's easy enough. He lost fifty dollars and the boots."

"I don't think that's quite right," said James, smiling.

"Of course it is. Didn't he have to pay back fifty dollars in good money, and didn't the man walk off with the boots?"

"That's true; but he neither lost nor made by changing the bill. He received fifty dollars in good money and paid back the same, didn't he?"

"Yes."

"Whatever he lost his customer made, didn't he?"

"Yes."

"Well, the man walked off with forty-five dollars and a pair of boots. The other five dollars the shoemaker kept himself."

"That's so, Jim. I see it now, but it's rather puzzling at first. Did you make that out yourself?"

"Yes."

"Then you've got a good head—better than I expected. Have you got any more questions?"

"Just a few."

So the boy continued to ask questions, and the captain was more than once obliged to confess that he could not answer. He began to form a new opinion of his young cousin, who, though he filled the humble position of a canal-boy, appeared to be well equipped with knowledge.

"I guess that'll do, Jim," he said after a while. "You've got ahead of me, though I didn't expect it. A boy with such a head as you've got ought not to be on the tow-path."

"What ought I to be doing, cousin?"

"You ought to keep school. You're better qualified than I am to-day, and yet I taught for three winters in Indiana."

James was pleased with this tribute to his acquirements, especially from a former schoolmaster.

"I never thought of that," he said. "I'm too young to keep school. I'm only fifteen."

"That is rather young. You know enough; but I aint sure that you could tackle some of the big boys that would be coming to school. You know enough, but you need more muscle. I'll tell you what I advise. Stay with me this summer—it won't do you any hurt, and you'll be earning something—then go to school a term or two, and by that time you'll be qualified to teach a district school."

"I'll think of what you say, cousin," said James, thoughtfully. "I don't know but your advice is good."

It is not always easy to say what circumstances have most influence in shaping the destiny of a boy, but it seems probable that the conversation which has just been detailed, and the discovery that he was quite equal in knowledge to a man who had been a schoolmaster, may have put new ideas into the boy's head, destined to bear fruit later.

For the present, however, his duties as a canal-boy must be attended to, and they were soon to be resumed.

About ten o'clock that night, when James was on duty, the boat approached the town of Akron, where there were twenty-one locks to be successively passed through.

The night was dark, and, though the bowman of the *Evening Star* did not see it, another boat had reached the same lock from the opposite direction. Now in such cases the old rule, "first come, first served," properly prevailed.

The bowman had directed the gates to be thrown open, in order that the boat might enter the lock, when a voice was heard through the darkness, "Hold on, there! Our boat is just round the bend, ready to enter."

"We have as much right as you," said the bowman.

As he spoke he commenced turning the gate.

My young reader will understand from the description already given that it will not do to have both lower and upper gates open at the same time. Of course, one or the other boat must wait.

Both bowmen were determined to be first, and neither was willing to yield. Both boats were near the lock, their head-lights shining as bright as day, and the spirit of antagonism reached and affected the crews of both.

Captain Letcher felt called upon to interfere lest there should be serious trouble.

He beckoned to his bowman.

"Were you here first?" he asked.

"It is hard to tell," answered the bowman, "but I'm bound to have the lock, anyhow."

The captain was not wholly unaffected by the spirit of antagonism which his bowman displayed.

"All right; just as you say," he answered, and it seemed likely that conflict was inevitable.

James Garfield had been an attentive observer, and an attentive listener to what had been said. He had formed his own ideas of what was right to be done.

"Look here, captain," he said, tapping Captain Letcher on the arm, "does this lock belong to us?"

"I really suppose, according to law, it does not; but we will have it, anyhow."

"No, we will not," replied the boy.

"And why not?" asked the captain, naturally surprised at such a speech from his young driver.

"Because it does not belong to us."

The captain was privately of opinion that the
boy was right, yet but for his remonstrance he
would have stood out against the claims of the
rival boat. He took but brief time for considerations, and announced his decision.

"Boys," he said to his men, "Jim is right. Let
them have the lock."

Of course there was no more trouble, but the
bowman, and the others connected with the *Evening Star*, were angry. It irritated them to be
obliged to give up the point, and wait humbly till
the other boat had passed through the lock.

The steersman was George Lee. When breakfast was called, he sat down by James.

"What is the matter with you, Jim?" he asked.

"Nothing at all."

"What made you so for giving up the lock last
night?"

"Because it wasn't ours. The other boat had it
by right."

"Jim, you are a coward," said Lee contemptu-
ously. "You aint fit for a boatman. You'd better go
back to the farm and chop wood or milk cows, for
a man or boy isn't fit for this business that isn't
ready to fight for his rights."

James did not answer. Probably he saw that it
would be of no use. George Lee was for his own
boat, right or wrong; but James had already begun to reflect upon the immutable principles of
right or wrong, and he did not suffer his reason to
be influenced by any considerations touching his
own interests or his own pride.

As to the charge of cowardice it did not trouble him much. On a suitable occasion later on (we shall tell the story in due season) he showed that he was willing to contend for his rights, when he was satisfied that the right was on his side.

CHAPTER VI.
JAMES LEAVES THE CANAL.

James was not long to fill the humble position of driver. Before the close of the first trip he was promoted to the more responsible office of bowman. Whether his wages were increased we are not informed.

It may be well in this place to mention that a canal boat required, besides the captain, two drivers, two steersmen, a bowman, and a cook, the last perhaps not the least important of the seven. "The bowman's business was to stop the boat as it entered the lock, by throwing the bowline that was attached to the bow of the boat around the snubbing post." It was to this position that James was promoted, though I have some doubt whether the place of driver, with the opportunities it afforded of riding on horse or mule-back, did not suit him better. Still, promotion is always pleasant, and in this case it showed that the boy had discharged his humbler duties satisfactorily.

I have said that the time came when James showed that he was not a coward. Edmund Kirke, in his admirable life of Garfield, has condensed the captain's account of the occurrence, and I quote it here as likely to prove interesting to my boy readers:

The *Evening Star* was at Beaver, and a steamboat was ready to tow her up to Pittsburg. The boy was standing on deck with the selting-pole against his shoulders, and some feet away stood Murphy, one of the boat hands, a big, burly fellow of thirty-five, when the steamboat threw the line, and, owing to a sudden lurch of the boat, it whirled over the boy's head, and flew in the direction of the boatman. "Look out, Murphy!" cried the boy; but the rope had anticipated him, and knocked Murphy's hat off into the river. The boy expressed his regret, but it was of no avail. In a towering rage the man rushed upon him, with his head down, like a maddened animal; but, stepping nimbly aside, the boy dealt him a powerful blow behind the ear, and he tumbled to the bottom of the boat among the copper ore. Before he could rise the boy was upon him, one hand upon his throat, the other raised for another blow upon his frontispiece.

"Pound the cussed fool, Jim!" cried Captain Letcher, who was looking on appreciatingly. "If he haint no more sense'n to get mad at accidents, giv it ter him! Why don't you strike?"

But the boy did not strike, for the man was down and in his power. Murphy expressed regret for his rage, and then Garfield gave him his hand, and they became better friends than ever before. This victory of a boy of sixteen over a man of thirty-five obliterated the notion of young Garfield's character for cowardice, and gave him a great reputation among his associates. The incident is still well remembered among the boatmen of the Ohio and Pennsylvania Canal.

The boy's speedy reconciliation to the man who had made so unprovoked an assault upon him was characteristic of his nature. He never could cherish malice, and it was very hard work for him to remain angry with any one, however great the provocation.

Both as a boy and as a man he possessed great physical strength, as may be inferred from an incident told by the Boston *Journal* of his life when he was no longer the humble canal-boy, but a brigadier-general in the army:

At Pittsburg Landing one night in 1862 there was a rush for rations by some newly-arrived troops. One strong, fine-looking soldier presented a requisition for a barrel of flour, *and, shouldering it, walked off with ease.* When the wagon was loaded, this same man stepped up to Colonel Morton, commanding the commissary steamers there, and remarked, "I suppose you require a receipt for these supplies?"

"Yes," said the Colonel, as he handed over the usual blank; "just take this provision return, and have it signed by your commanding officer."

"Can't I sign it?" was the reply.

"Oh, no," said the affable Colonel Morton; "it requires the signature of a commissioned officer."

Then came the remark, that still remains fresh in the Colonel's memory: "I am a commissioned officer—I'm a brigadier-general, and my name is Garfield, of Ohio."

For four months James remained connected with the canal-boat. To show that traveling by canal is not so free from danger as it is supposed to be, it may be stated that in this short time he fell into the water fourteen times. Usually he scrambled out without further harm than a good wetting. One night, however, he was in serious pain.

It was midnight, and rainy, when he was called up to take his turn at the bow. The boat was leaving one of those long reaches of slack-water which abound in the Ohio and Pennsylvania Canal. He tumbled out of bed in a hurry, but half awake, and, taking his stand on the narrow platform below the bow-deck, he began uncoiling a rope to steady the boat through a lock it was approaching. Finally it knotted, and caught in a narrow cleft on the edge of the deck. He gave it a strong pull, then another, till it gave way, sending him over the bow into the water. Down he went in the dark river, and, rising, was bewildered amid the intense darkness. It seemed as if the boy's brief career was at its close. But he was saved as by a miracle. Reaching out his hand in the darkness, it came in contact with the rope. Holding firmly to it as it tightened in his grasp, he used his strong arms to draw himself up hand over hand. His deliverance was due to a knot in the rope catching in a crevice, thus, as it tightened, sustaining him and enabling him to climb on deck.

It was a narrow escape, and he felt it to be so. He was a thoughtful boy, and it impressed him. The chances had been strongly against him, yet he had been saved.

"God did it," thought James reverently, "He has saved my life against large odds, and He must have saved it for some purpose. He has some work for me to do."

Few boys at his age would have taken the matter so seriously, yet in the light of after events shall we not say that James was right, and that God did have some work for him to perform?

This work, the boy decided, was not likely to be the one he was at present engaged in. The work of a driver or a bowman on a canal is doubtless useful in its way, but James doubted whether he would be providentially set apart for any such business.

It might have been this deliverance that turned his attention to religious matters. At any rate, hearing that at Bedford there was a series of protracted meetings conducted by the Disciples, as they were called, he made a trip there, and became seriously impressed. There, too, he met a gentleman who was destined to exert an important influence over his destiny.

This gentleman was Dr. J.P. Robinson, who may be still living. Dr. Robinson took a great liking to the boy, and sought to be of service to him. He employed him, though it may have been at a later period, to chop wood, and take care of his garden, and do chores about the house, and years afterward, as we shall see, it was he that enabled James to enter Williams College, and pursue his studies there until he graduated, and was ready to do the work of an educated man in the world. But we must not anticipate.

Though James was strong and healthy he was not proof against the disease that lurked in the low lands bordering on the canal. He was attacked by fever and ague, and lay for some months sick at home. It was probably the only long sickness he had till the fatal wound which laid him on his bed when in the fullness of his fame he had taken his place among kings and rulers. It is needless to say that he had every attention that a tender mother could bestow, and in time he was restored to health.

During his sickness he had many talks with his mother upon his future prospects, and the course of life upon which it was best for him to enter. He had not yet given up all thoughts of the sea, he had not forgotten the charms with which a sailor's life is invested in Marryatt's fascinating novels. His mother listened anxiously to his dreams of happiness on the sea, and strove to fix his mind upon higher things—to inspire him with a nobler ambition.

"What would you have me do, mother?" he asked.

"If you go back to the canal, my son, with the

seeds of this disease lurking in your system, I fear you will be taken down again. I have thought it over. It seems to me you had better go to school this spring, and then, with a term in the fall, you may be able to teach in the winter. If you teach winters, and work on the canal or lake summers, you will have employment the year round."

Nevertheless Mrs. Garfield was probably not in favor of his spending his summers in the way indicated. She felt, however, that her son, who was a boy like other boys, must be gradually weaned from the dreams that had bewitched his fancy.

Then his mother proposed a practical plan.

"You have been obliged to spend all your money," she said, "but your brother Thomas and I will be able to raise seventeen dollars for you to start to school on, and when that is gone perhaps you will be able to get along on your own resources."

CHAPTER VII.
THE CHOICE OF A VOCATION.

James Garfield's experience on the canal was over. The position was such an humble one that it did not seem likely to be of any service in the larger career which one day was to open before him. But years afterward, when as a brigadier-general of volunteers he made an expedition into Eastern Kentucky, he realized advantage from his four months' experience on the canal. His command had run short of provisions, and a boat had been sent for supplies, but the river beside which the men were encamped had risen so high that the boat dared not attempt to go up the river. Then General Garfield, calling to his aid the skill with which he had guided the *Evening Star* at the age of fifteen, took command of the craft, stood at the wheel forty-four hours out of the forty-eight, and brought the supplies to his men at a time when they were eating their last crackers.

"Seek all knowledge, however trifling," says an eminent author, "and there will come a time when you can make use of it."

James may never have read this remark, but he was continually acting upon it, and the spare moments which others devoted to recreation he used in adding to his stock of general knowledge.

The last chapter closes with Mrs. Garfield's advice to James to give up his plan of going to sea, and to commence and carry forward a course of education which should qualify him for a college professor, or a professional career. Her words made some impression upon his mind, but it is not always easy to displace cherished dreams. While she was talking, a knock was heard at the door and Mrs. Garfield, leaving her place at her son's bedside, rose and opened it.

"I am glad to see you, Mr. Bates," she said with a welcoming smile.

Samuel D. Bates was the teacher of the school near by, an earnest young man, of exemplary habits, who was looking to the ministry as his chosen vocation.

"And how is James to-day?" asked the teacher, glancing toward the bed.

"So well that he is already beginning to make

plans for the future," answered his mother.

"What are your plans, James?" asked the young man.

"I should like best to go to sea," said James, "but mother doesn't approve of it."

"She is wise," said Bates, promptly. "You would find it a great disappointment."

"But, it must be delightful to skim over the waters, and visit countries far away," said the boy, his cheeks flushing, and his eyes glowing with enthusiasm.

"You think so now; but remember, you would be a poor, ignorant sailor, and would have to stay by the ship instead of exploring the wonderful cities at which the ship touched. Of course, you would have an occasional run on shore, but you could not shake off the degrading associations with which your life on shipboard would surround you."

"Why should a sailor's life be degrading?" asked James.

"It need not be necessarily, but as a matter of fact most sailors have low aims and are addicted to bad habits. Better wait till you can go to sea as a passenger, and enjoy to the full the benefits of foreign travel."

"There is something in that," said James, thoughtfully. "If I could only be sure of going some day."

"Wouldn't it be pleasant to go as a man of culture, as a college professor, as a minister, or as a lawyer, able to meet on equal terms foreign scholars and gentlemen?"

This was a new way of putting it, and produced a favorable impression on the boy's mind. Still, the boy had doubts, and expressed them freely.

"That sounds well," he said; "but how am I to know that I have brain enough to make a college professor, or a minister, or a lawyer?"

"I don't think there is much doubt on that point," said Bates, noting the bright, expressive face, and luminous eyes of the sick boy. "I should be willing to guarantee your capacity. Don't you think yourself fit for anything better than a common sailor?"

"Yes," answered James. "I think I could make a good carpenter, for I know something about that trade already, and I daresay I could make a good trader if I could find an opening to learn the business; but it takes a superior man to succeed in the positions you mention."

"There are plenty of men with only average ability who get along very creditably; but I advise you, if you make up your mind to enter the lists, to try for a high place."

The boy's eyes sparkled with new ambition. It was a favorite idea with him afterward, that every man ought to feel an honorable ambition to succeed as well as possible in his chosen path.

"One thing more," added Bates. "I don't think you have any right to become a sailor."

"No right? Oh, you mean because mother objects."

"That, certainly, ought to weigh with you as a good son; but I referred to something else."

"What then?"

"Do you remember the parable of the talents?"

James had been brought up by his mother, who was a devoted religious woman, to read the Bible, and he answered in the affirmative.

"It seems to me that you are responsible for the talents which God has bestowed upon you. If you have the ability or the brain, as you call it, to insure success in a literary career, don't you think you would throw yourself away if you became a sailor?"

Mrs. Garfield, who had listened with deep interest to the remarks of the young man, regarded James anxiously, to see what effect these arguments were having upon him. She did not fear disobedience. She knew that if she should make it a personal request, James was dutiful enough to follow her wishes; but she respected the personal independence of her children, and wanted to convince, rather than to coerce, them.

"If I knew positively that you were right in your estimate of me, Mr. Bates, I would go in for a course of study."

"Consult some one in whose judgment you have confidence, James," said the teacher, promptly.

"Can you suggest any one?" asked the boy.

"Yes, Dr. J.P. Robinson, of Bedford, is visiting at the house of President Hayden, of Hiram College. You have heard of him?"

"Yes."

"He is a man of ripe judgment, and you can

rely implicitly on what he says."

"As soon as I am well enough I will do as you advise," said James.

"Then I am satisfied. I am sure the doctor will confirm my advice."

"Mr. Bates," said Mrs. Garfield, as she followed out the young teacher, "I am much indebted to you for your advice to James. It is in accordance with my wishes. If he should decide to obtain an education, where would you advise him to go?"

"To the seminary where I have obtained all the education I possess," answered the young man.

"Where is it?"

"It is called the 'Geauga Seminary,' and is located in Chester, in the next county. For a time it will be sufficient to meet all James' needs. When he is further advanced he can go to Hiram College."

"Is it expensive?" asked Mrs. Garfield. "James has no money except the few dollars his brother and I can spare him."

"He will have plenty of company. Most of the students are poor, but there are chances of finding work in the neighborhood, and so earning a little money. James knows something of the carpenter's trade?"

"Yes, he helped build the house we live in, and he has been employed on several barns."

My readers will remember that the Garfields no longer lived in the humble log-cabin in which we first found them. The money Thomas brought home from Michigan, supplemented by the labor of James and himself, had replaced it by a neat frame house, which was much more comfortable and sightly.

"That will do. I think I know a man who will give him employment."

"He is a boy of energy. If he gets fairly started at school, I think he will maintain himself there," said Mrs. Garfield.

The teacher took his leave.

When Mrs. Garfield re-entered the room she found James looking very thoughtful.

"Mother," he said, abruptly, "I want to get well as quick as I can. I am sixteen years old, and it is time I decided what to do with myself."

"You will think of what Mr. Bates has said, will you not?"

"Yes, mother; as soon as I am well enough I will call on Dr. Robinson and ask his candid opinion. I will be guided by what he says."

CHAPTER VIII.
GEAUGA SEMINARY.

I have stated in a previous chapter that James became acquainted with Dr. Robinson while still employed on the canal. This statement was made on the authority of Mr. Philo Chamberlain, of Cleveland, who was part proprietor of the line of canal-boats on which the boy was employed. Edmund Kirke, however, conveys the impression that James was a stranger to the doctor at the time he called upon him after his sickness. Mr. Kirke's information having been derived chiefly from General Garfield himself, I shall adopt hi version, as confirmed by Dr. Robinson.

When James walked up to the residence of President Hayden, and inquired for Dr. Robinson, he was decidedly homespun in appearance. He probably was dressed in his best, but his best was shabby enough. His trousers were of coarse satinet, and might have fitted him a season or two before, but now were far outgrown, reaching only half-way down from the tops of his cowhide boots. His waistcoat also was much too short, and his coat was threadbare, the sleeves being so short as to display a considerable portion of his arms. Add to these a coarse slouched hat, much the worse for wear, and a heavy mass of yellow hair much too long, and we can easily understand what the good doctor said of him: "He was wonderfully awkward, but had a sort of independent, go-as-you-please manner that impressed me favorably."

"Who are you?" asked the doctor.

"My name is James Garfield, from Solon."

"Oh, I know your mother, and knew you when you were a babe, but you have outgrown my knowledge. I am glad to see you."

"I should like to see you alone," said James.

The doctor led the way to a secluded spot in the neighborhood of the house, and then, sitting down on a log, the youth, after a little hesitation, opened his business.

"You are a physician," he said, "and know the fiber that is in men. Examine me and tell me with the utmost frankness whether I had better take a course of liberal study. I am contemplating doing so, as my desire is in that direction. But if I am to make a failure of it, or practically so, I do not desire to begin. If you advise me not to do so I shall be content."

In speaking of this incident the doctor has remarked recently: "I felt that I was on my sacred honor, and the young man looked as though he felt himself on trial. I had had considerable experience as a physician, but here was a case much different from any I had ever had. I felt that it must be handled with great care. I examined his head and saw that there was a magnificent brain there. I sounded his lungs, and found that they were strong, and capable of making good blood. I felt his pulse, and felt that there was an engine capable of sending the blood up to the head to feed the brain. I had seen many strong physical systems with warm feet and cold, sluggish brain; and those who possessed such systems would simply sit round and doze. Therefore I was anxious to know about the kind of an engine to run that delicate machine, the brain. At the end of a fifteen minutes' careful examination of this kind, we rose, and I said:

"Go on, follow the leadings of your ambition, and ever after I am your friend. You have the brain of a Webster, and you have the physical proportions that will back you in the most herculean efforts. All you need to do is to work; work hard, do not be afraid of over-working and you will make your mark."

It will be easily understood that these words from a man whom he held in high respect were enough to fix the resolution of James. If he were really so well fitted for the work and the career which his mother desired him to follow, it was surely his duty to make use of the talents which he had just discovered were his.

After that there was no more question about going to sea. He deliberately decided to become a scholar, and then follow where Providence led the way.

He would have liked a new suit of clothes, but this was out of the question. All the money he had at command was the seventeen dollars which his mother had offered him. He must get along with this sum, and so with hopeful heart he set out for Geauga Seminary.

He did not go alone. On hearing of his determination, two boys, one a cousin, made up their minds to accompany him.

Possibly my young readers may imagine the scene of leave-taking, as the stage drove up to the door, and the boys with their trunks or valises were taken on board, but if so, imagination would picture a scene far different from the reality. Their outfit was of quite a different kind.

For the sake of economy the boys were to board themselves, and Mrs. Garfield with provident heart supplied James with a frying-pan, and a few necessary dishes, so that his body might not suffer while his mind was being fed. Such was the luxury that awaited James in his new home. I am afraid that the hearts of many of my young readers would sink within them if they thought that they must buy an education at such a cost as that. But let them not forget that this homespun boy, with his poor array of frying-pan and dishes, was years after to strive in legislative halls, and win the highest post in the gift of his fellow-citizens. And none of these things would have been his, in all likelihood, but for his early struggle with poverty.

So far as I know, neither of his companions was any better off than James. All three were young adventurers traveling into the domains of science with hopeful hearts and fresh courage, not altogether ignorant of the hardships that awaited them, but prepared to work hard for the prizes of knowledge.

Arrived at Geauga Seminary, they called upon the principal and announced for what purpose they had come.

"Well, young men, I hope you mean to work?" he said.

"Yes, sir," answered James promptly. "I am poor, and I want to get an education as quick as I can."

"I like your sentiments, and I will help you as far as I can."

The boys succeeded in hiring a room in an old unpainted building near the academy for a small weekly sum. It was unfurnished, but they succeeded in borrowing a few dilapidated chairs from a neighbor who did not require them, and some straw ticks, which they spread upon the floor for sleeping purposes. In one corner they stowed their frying-pans, kettles, and dishes, and then they set up housekeeping in humble style.

The Geauga Seminary was a Freewill Baptist institution, and was attended by a considerable number of students, to whom it did not, indeed, furnish what is called "the higher education," but it was a considerable advance upon any school that James had hitherto attended. English grammar, natural philosophy, arithmetic, and algebra—these were the principal studies to which James devoted himself, and they opened to him new fields of thought. Probably it was at this humble seminary that he first acquired the thirst for learning that ever afterward characterized him.

Let us look in upon the three boys a night or two after they have commenced housekeeping.

They take turns in cooking, and this time it is the turn of the one in whom we feel the strongest interest.

"What have we got for supper, boys?" he asks, for the procuring of supplies has fallen to them.

"Here are a dozen eggs," said Henry Bounton, his cousin.

"And here is a loaf of bread, which I got at the baker's," said his friend.

"That's good! We'll have bread and fried eggs. There is nothing better than that."

"Eggs have gone up a cent a dozen," remarks Henry, gravely.

This news is received seriously, for a cent means something to them. Probably even then the price was not greater than six to eight cents a dozen, for prices were low in the West at that time.

"Then we can't have them so often," said James, philosophically, "unless we get something to do."

"There's a carpenter's-shop a little way down the street," said Henry. "I guess you can find employment there."

"I'll go round there after supper."

Meanwhile he attended to his duty as cook, and in due time each of the boys was supplied with four fried eggs and as much bread as he cared for. Probably butter was dispensed with, as too costly a luxury, until more prosperous times.

When supper was over the boys took a walk, and then, returning to their humble room, spent the evening in preparing their next morning's lessons.

In them James soon took leading rank, for his brain was larger, and his powers of application and intuition great, as Dr. Robinson had implied. From the time he entered Geauga Seminary probably he never seriously doubted that he had entered upon the right path.

CHAPTER IX.
WAYS AND MEANS.

James called on the carpenter after supper and inquired if he could supply him with work.

"I may be able to if you are competent," was the reply. "Have you ever worked at the business?"

"Yes."

"Where?"

"At Orange, where my home is."

"How long did you work at it?"

"Perhaps I had better tell you what I have done," said James.

He then gave an account of the barns he had been employed upon, and the frame house which he had assisted to build for his mother.

"I don't set up for a first-class workman," he added, with a smile, "but I think I can be of some use to you."

"I will try you, for I am rather pressed with work just now."

So, in a day or two James was set to work.

The carpenter found that it was as he had represented. He was not a first-class workman. Indeed, he had only a rudimentary knowledge of the trade, but he was quick to learn, and in a short time he was able to help in many ways. His wages were not very large, but they were satisfactory, since they enabled him to pay his expenses and keep his head above water. Before the seventeen dollars were exhausted, he had earned quite a sum by his labor in the carpenter's-shop.

About this time he received a letter from his brother.

"Dear James," he wrote, "I shall be glad to hear how you are getting along. You took so little money with you that you may need more. If so, let me know, and I will try to send you some."

James answered promptly: "Don't feel anxious about me, Thomas. I have been fortunate enough to secure work at a carpenter's-shop, and my expenses of living are very small. I intend not to call upon you or mother again, but to pay my own way, if I keep my health."

He kept his word, and from that time did not find it necessary to call either upon his mother or his good brother, who was prepared to make personal sacrifices, as he had been doing all his life, that his younger brother might enjoy advantages which he had to do without.

At length the summer vacation came. James had worked hard and won high rank in his respective studies. He had a robust frame, and he seemed never to get tired. No doubt he took especial interest in composition and the exercises of the debating society which flourished at Geauga, as at most seminaries of advanced education. In after-life he was so ready and powerful in debate, that we can readily understand that he must have begun early to try his powers. Many a trained speaker has first come to a consciousness of his strength in a lyceum of boys, pitted against some school-fellow of equal attainments. No doubt many crude and some ludicrous speeches are made by boys in their teens, but at least they learn to think on their feet, and acquire the ability to stand the gaze of an audience without discomposure. A certain easy facility of expression also is gained, which enables them to acquit themselves creditably on a more important stage.

James early learned that the best preparation for a good speech is a thorough familiarity with the subject, and in his after-life he always carefully prepared himself, so that he was a forcible debater, whom it was not easy to meet and conquer.

"He once told me how he prepared his speeches," said Representative Williams, of Wisconsin, since his death. "First he filled himself with the subject, massing all the facts and principles involved, so far as he could; then he took pen and paper and wrote down the salient points in what he regarded their logical order. Then he scanned these critically, and fixed them in his memory. 'And then,' said he, 'I leave the paper in my room and trust to the emergency.'"

When the vacation came James began to look about for work. He could not afford to be idle. Moreover, he hoped to be able to earn enough that he might not go back empty-handed in the fall.

Generally work comes to him who earnestly seeks it, and James heard of a man who wanted some wood cut.

He waited upon this man and questioned him about it.

"Yes," he answered, "I want the wood cut. What will you charge to do it?"

"How much is there?"

"About a hundred cords."

James thought of the time when he cut twenty-five cords for seven dollars, and he named a price to correspond.

"I'll give you twenty-five dollars," said the proprietor of the wood.

It was a low price for the labor involved, but, on the other hand, it would be of essential service to the struggling student.

"I will undertake it," he said.

"When will you go to work?"

"Now!" answered James promptly.

How long it took him to do the work we have no record, but he doubtless worked steadfastly till it was accomplished. We can imagine the satisfaction he felt when the money was put into his hands, and he felt that he would not need to be quite so economical in the coming term.

Accordingly, when the vacation was over and James went back to the seminary, he did not re-engage the room which he and his two friends had rented the term before. He realized that to be in a condition to study well he must feed his body well, and he was in favor of a more generous system of diet. Besides, the labor required for cooking was so much time taken from his study hours.

He heard that a widow—Mrs. Stiles—mother of the present sheriff of Ashtabula County, was prepared to receive boarders, and, accordingly, he called upon her to ascertain if she would receive him.

She knew something of him already, for she learned that he had obtained the reputation of a steady and orderly student, and was disposed to favor his application.

The next question was an important one to young Garfield.

"How much do you expect me to pay?"

He waited with some anxiety for the answer, for though he had twenty-five dollars in his pocket, the term was a long one, and tuition was to be paid also.

"A dollar and six cents will be about right,"

said Mrs. Stiles, "for board, washing, and lodging."

"That will be satisfactory," said James, with a sigh of relief, for he saw his way clear to pay this sum for a time, at least, and for the whole term if he could again procure employment at his old trade.

A dollar and six cents! It was rather an odd sum, and we should consider it nowadays as very low for any sort of board in any village, however obscure or humble. But in those days it was not so exceptional, and provisions were so much lower that the widow probably lost nothing by her boarder, though she certainly could not have made much.

James had no money to spare for another purpose, though there was need enough of it. He needed some new clothes badly. He had neither underclothing nor overcoat, and but one outside suit, of cheap Kentucky jean. No doubt he was subjected to mortification on account of his slender supply of clothing. At any rate he was once placed in embarrassing circumstances.

Toward the close of the term, as Mrs. Stiles says, his trowsers became exceedingly thin at the knees, and one unlucky day, when he was incautiously bending forward, they tore half-way round the leg, exposing his bare knee.

James was very much mortified, and repaired damages as well as he could with a pin.

"I need a new suit of clothes badly," he said in the evening, "but I can't afford to buy one. See how I have torn my trowsers."

"Oh, that is easy enough to mend," said Mrs. Stiles, cheerfully.

"But I have no other pair to wear while they are being mended," said James, with a blush.

"Then you must go to bed early, and send them down by one of the boys. I will darn the hole so that you will never know it. You won't mind such trifles when you become President."

It was a jocose remark, and the good lady little dreamed that, in after years, the young man with but one pair of pantaloons, and those more than half worn, would occupy the proud position she referred to.

CHAPTER X.
A COUSIN'S REMINISCENCES.

During his school-life at Geauga Seminary James enjoyed the companionship of a cousin, Henry B. Boynton, who still lives on the farm adjoining the one on which our hero was born. The relationship between the two boys was much closer than is common between cousins; for while their mothers were sisters, their fathers were half-brothers. Henry was two years older than James, and they were more like brothers than cousins. I am sure my young readers will be glad to read what Henry has to say of their joint school-life. I quote from the account of an interview held with a correspondent of the Boston *Herald*, bearing the date of September 23, 1881:

When General Garfield was nominated to the Presidency his old neighbors in Orange erected a flag-staff where the house stood which Garfield and his brother erected for their mother and sisters with their own hands, after the log hut, a little farther out in the field nearer the wood, had become unfit for habitation. Thomas Garfield, the uncle of the President, who not long since was killed by a railroad accident, directed the manual labor of rearing the shaft, and was proud of his work.

There is nothing except this hole left to mark his birth-place, and the old well, not two rods off, which he and his brother dug to furnish water for the family. In the little maple grove to the left, children played about the school-house where the dead President first gathered the rudiments upon which he built to such purpose. The old orchard in its sere and yellow leaf, the dying grass, and the turning maple leaves seemed to join in the great mourning.

Adjoining the field where the flag floats is an unpretentious home, almost as much identified with Gen. Garfield's early history as the one he helped to clear of the forest timber while he was yet but a child. It is the home of Henry B. Boynton, cousin of the dead President, and a brother of Dr. Boynton, whose name has become so well known from recent events.

While rambling over this place the correspondent came upon this near relative of Garfield, smaller in stature than he was, but in features bearing a striking resemblance to him.

"General Garfield and I were like brothers," he said, as he turned from giving some directions to his farm hands, now sowing the fall grain upon ground which his cousin had first helped to break. "His father died yonder, within a stone's throw of us, when the son was but a year and a half old. He knew no other father than mine, who watched over the family as if it had been his own. This very house in which I live was as much his home as it was mine.

"Over there," said he, pointing to the brick school-house in the grove of maples, around which the happy children were playing, "is where he and I both started for school. I have read a statement that he could not read or write until he was nineteen. He could do both before he was nine, and before he was twelve, so familiar was he with the Indian history of the country, that he had named every tree in the orchard, which his father planted as he was born, with the name of some Indian chief, and even debated in societies, religion, and other topics with men. One favorite tree of his he named Tecumseh, and the branches of many of these old trees have been cut since his promotion to the Presidency by relic-hunters, and carried away.

"Gen. Garfield was a remarkable boy as well as man. It is not possible to tell you the fight he made amid poverty for a place in life, and how gradually he obtained it. When he was a boy he would rather read than work. But he became a great student. He had to work after he was twelve years of age. In those days we were all poor, and it took hard knocks to get on. He worked clearing the fields yonder with his brother, and then cut cord-wood, and did other farm labor to get the necessities of life for his mother and sisters.

"I remember when he was fourteen years of age, he went away to work at Daniel Morse's, not four miles down the road from here, and after the labors of the day he sat down to listen to the conversation of a teacher in one of the schools of Cleveland, when it was yet a village, who had called. The talk of the educated man pleased the boy, and, while intent upon his story, a daughter of the man for whom he was working informed the future President with great dignity that it was time that *servants* were in bed, and that she preferred his absence to his presence.

"Nothing that ever happened to him so severely stung him as this affront. In his youth he could never refer to it without indignation, and almost immediately he left Mr. Morse's employ and went on the canal. He said to me then that those people should live to see the day when they would not care to insult him.

"His experience on the canal was a severe one, but perhaps useful. I can remember the winter when he came home after the sum-

mer's service there. He had the chills all that
fall and winter, yet he would shake and get his
lessons at home; go over to the school and recite, and thus keep up with his class. The next
spring found him weak from constant ague.
Yet he intended to return to the canal.

"Here came the turning-point in his life.
Mr. Bates, who taught the school, pleaded
with him not to do so, and said that if he would
continue in school till the next fall he could get
a certificate. I received a certificate about the
same time. The next year we went to the seminary at Chester, only twelve miles distant.
Here our books were furnished us, and we
cooked our own victuals. We lived upon a dollar a week each. Our diet was strong, but very
plain; mush and molasses, pork and potatoes.
Saturdays we took our axes, and went into the
woods and cut cord-wood. During vacations
we labored in the harvest-field, or taught a
district school, as we could.

"Yonder," said he, pointing to a beautiful valley, about two miles distant, "stands
the school-house where Garfield first taught
school. He got twelve dollars a month, and
boarded round. I also taught school in a neighboring town. We both went back to Chester to
college, and would probably have finished our
education there, but it was a Baptist school,
and they were constantly making flings at the
children of the Disciples, and teaching sectar-
ianism. As the Disciples grew stronger they
determined their children should not be sub-

jected to such influence; the college of our own Church was established at Hiram, and there Garfield and I went."

Though the remainder of the reminiscences somewhat anticipate the course of our story, it is perhaps as well to insert it here.

"We lodged in the basement most of the time, and boarded at the present Mrs. Garfield's father's house. During our school-days here I nursed the late President through an attack of the measles which nearly ended his life. He has often said, that, were it not for my attention, he could not have lived. So you see that the General and myself were very close to one another from the time either of us could lisp until he became President. Here is a picture we had taken together," showing an old daguerreotype. "It does not resemble either of us much now. And yet they do say that we bore in our childhood, and still bear, a striking resemblance. I am still a farmer, while he grew great and powerful. He never permitted a suggestion, however, to be made in my presence as to the difference in our paths of life. He visited me here before election, and looked with gratification upon that pole yonder, and its flag, erected by his neighbors and kinsmen. He wandered over the fields he had himself helped clear and pointed out to me trees from the limbs of which he had shot squirrel after squirrel, and beneath the branches of which he had played and worked in the years of his infancy and boyhood.

"I forgot to say that one of Gen. Garfield's striking characteristics while he was growing up, was, that when he saw a boy in the class excel him in anything, he never gave up till he reached the same standard, and even went beyond it. It got to be known that no scholar could be ahead of him. Our association as men has been almost as close as that of our boyhood, though not as constant. The General never forgot his neighbors or less fortunate kinsmen, and often visited us as we did him."

More vivid than any picture I could draw is this description, by the most intimate friend of his boyhood, of James Garfield's way of life, his struggles for an education, his constant desire to excel, and his devotion to duty. We have already pictured the rustic boy in his humble room, cooking his own food, and living, as his cousin testifies, on a dollar a week. Is there any other country where such humble beginnings could lead to such influence and power? Is there any other land where such a lad could make such rapid strides toward the goal which crowns the highest ambition? It is the career of such men that most commends our Government and institutions, proving as it does that by the humblest and poorest the highest dignities may be attained. James was content to live on mush and molasses, pork and potatoes, since they came within his narrow means, and gave him sufficient strength to pursue his cherished studies. Nor is his an exceptional case. I have myself known college and professional students who have lived on sixty cents a week (how, it is difficult to tell), while their minds were busy with the loftiest problems that have ever engaged the human intellect. Such boys and young men are the promise of the republic. They toil upwards while others sleep, and many such have written their names high on the tablets in the Temple of Fame.

CHAPTER XI.
LEDGE HILL SCHOOL

Ever since he began to study at Geauga Seminary James had looked forward to earning a little money by keeping school himself; not an advanced school, of course, but an ordinary school, such as was kept in the country districts in the winter. He felt no hesitation as to his competence. The qualifications required by the school committees were by no means large, and so far there was no difficulty.

There was one obstacle, however: James was still a boy himself—a large boy, to be sure, but he had a youthful face, and the chances were that he would have a number of pupils older than himself. Could he keep order? Would the rough country boys submit to the authority of one like themselves, whatever might be his reputation as a scholar? This was a point to consider anxiously. However, James had pluck, and he was ready to try the experiment.

He would have been glad to secure a school

so far away that he could go there as a stranger, and be received as a young man. But no such opportunity offered. There was another opening nearer home.

A teacher was wanted for the Ledge Hill district in Orange, and the committee-man bethought himself of James Garfield.

So one day he knocked at Mrs. Garfield's door.

"Is James at home?" he asked.

James heard the question, and came forward to meet his visitor.

"Good-morning," he said, pleasantly; "did you want to see me?"

"Are you calculating to keep school this winter" asked his visitor.

"If I can get a school to keep," was the reply.

"That's the business I came about. We want a schoolmaster for the Ledge Hill School. How would you like to try it?"

"The Ledge Hill School!" repeated James, in some dismay. "Why, all the boys know me there."

"Of course they do. Then they won't need to be introduced."

"Will they obey me? That's what I was thinking of. There are some pretty hard cases in that school."

"That's where you are right."

"I wouldn't like to try it and fail," said James, doubtfully.

"You won't if you'll follow my advice," said the committee-man.

"What's that?"

"Thrash the first boy that gives you any trou-

ble. Don't half do it; but give him a sound flog-
ging, so that he will understand who's master.
You're strong enough; you can do it."

James extended his muscular arm with a
smile. He knew he was strong. He was a large
boy, and his training had been such as to develop
his muscles.

"You know the boys that will go to school. Is
there any one that can master you?" asked his
visitor.

"No, I don't think there is," answered James,
with a smile.

"Then you'll do. Let 'em know you are not
afraid of them the first day. That's the best advice
I can give you."

"I shouldn't like to get into a fight with a pupil," said James, slowly.

"You'll have to run the risk of it unless you
teach a girls' school. I guess you wouldn't have
any trouble there."

"Not of that kind, probably. What wages do
you pay?"

"Twelve dollars a month and board. Of course,
you'll board round."

Twelve dollars a month would not be considered very high wages now, but to James it was
a consideration. He had earned as much in other ways, but he was quite anxious to try his luck
as a teacher. That might be his future vocation,
not teaching a district school, of course, but this
would be the first round of the ladder that might
lead to a college professorship. The first step is
the most difficult, but it must be taken, and the

Ledge Hill School, difficult as it probably would be, was to be the first step for the future President of Hiram College.

All these considerations James rapidly revolved in his mind, and then he came to a decision.

"When does the school commence?" he asked.

"Next Monday."

"I accept your offer. I'll be on hand in time."

* * * * *

The news quickly reached the Ledge Hill district that "Jim Garfield," as he was popularly called, was to be their next teacher.

"Have you heard about the new master?" asked Tom Bassett, one of the hard cases, of a friend.

"No. Who is it?"

"Jim Garfield."

The other whistled.

"You don't mean it?"

"Yes, I do."

"How did you hear?"

"Mr. ——," naming the committee-man, "told me."

"Then it must be so. We'll have a high old time if that's so."

"So we will," chuckled the other. "I'm anxious for school to begin."

"He's only a boy like us."

"That's so."

"He knows enough for a teacher; but knowing isn't everything."

"You're right. We can't be expected to mind a boy like ourselves that we've known all our lives."

"Of course not."

"I like Jim well enough. He's a tip-top feller; but, all the same, he aint goin' to boss me round."

"Nor me, either."

This conversation between Tom Bassett and Bill Stackpole (for obvious reasons I use assumed names) augured ill for the success of the young teacher. They determined to make it hot for him, and have all the fun they wanted.

They thought they knew James Garfield, but they made a mistake. They knew that he was of a peaceable disposition and not fond of quarreling, and although they also knew that he was strong and athletic, they decided that he would not long be able to maintain his position. If they had been able to read the doubts and fears that agitated the mind of their future preceptor, they would have felt confirmed in their belief.

The fact was, James shrank from the ordeal that awaited him.

"If I were only going among strangers," he said to his mother, "I wouldn't mind it so much; but all these boys and girls have known me ever since I was a small boy and went barefoot."

"Does your heart fail you, my son?" asked his mother, who sympathized with him, yet saw that it was a trial which must come.

"I can't exactly say that, but I dread to begin."

"We must expect to encounter difficulties and perplexities, James. None of our lives run all smoothly. Shall we conquer them or let them conquer us?"

The boy's spirit was aroused.

"Say no more, mother," he replied. "I will undertake the school, and if success is any way possible, I will succeed. I have been shrinking from it, but I won't shrink any longer."

"That is the spirit that succeeds, James."

James laughed, and in answer quoted Campbell's stirring lines with proper emphasis:

I will victor exult, or in death be laid low,
With my face to the field and my feet to the foe.

So the time passed till the eventful day dawned on which James was to assume charge of his first school. He was examined, and adjudged to be qualified to teach; but that he anticipated in advance.

The building is still standing in which James taught his first school. It is used for quite another purpose now, being occupied as a carriage-house by the thrifty farmer who owns the ground upon which it stands. The place where the teacher's desk stood, behind which the boy stood as preceptor, is now occupied by two stalls for carriage-horses. The benches which once contained the children he taught have been removed to make room for the family carriage, and the playground is now a barnyard. The building sits upon a commanding eminence known as Ledge Hill, and overlooks a long valley winding between two lines of hills.

This description is furnished by the same correspondent of the Boston *Herald* to whom I am already indebted for Henry Boynton's reminiscences contained in the last chapter.

When James came in sight, and slowly ascended the hill in sight of the motley crew of boys and girls who were assembled in front of the schoolhouse on the first morning of the term, it was one of the most trying moments of his life. He knew instinctively that the boys were anticipating the fun in store for them in the inevitable conflict which awaited him, and he felt constrained and nervous. He managed, however, to pass through the crowd, wearing a pleasant smile and greeting his scholars with a bow. There was trouble coming, he was convinced, but he did not choose to betray any apprehension.

CHAPTER XII.
WHO SHALL BE MASTER?

With as much dignity as was possible under the circumstances, James stepped to the teacher's desk and rang the bell.

This was hardly necessary, for out of curiosity all the scholars had promptly followed the young teacher into the school-room and taken their seats.

After the introductory exercises, James made a brief address to the scholars:

"I don't need any introduction to you," he said, "for you all know me. I see before me many who have been my playfellows and associates, but to-day a new relation is established between us. I am here as your teacher, regularly appointed by the committee, and it is my duty to assist you as far as I can to increase your knowledge. I should hardly feel competent to do so if I had not lately attended Geauga Seminary, and thus improved my own education. I hope you will consider me a friend, not only as I have been, but as one who is interested in promoting your best interests. One thing more," he added, "it is not only my duty to teach you, but to maintain good order, and this I mean to do. In school I wish you to look upon me as your teacher, but outside I shall join you in your sports, and be as much a boy as any of you. We will now proceed to our daily lessons."

This speech was delivered with self-possession, and favorably impressed all who heard it, even the boys who meant to make trouble, but they could not give up their contemplated fun. Nevertheless, by tacit agreement, they preserved perfect propriety for the present. They were not ready for the explosion.

The boy teacher was encouraged by the unexpected quiet.

"After all," he thought, "everything is likely to go smoothly. I need not have troubled myself so much."

He knew the usual routine at the opening of a school term. The names of the children were to be taken, they were to be divided into classes, and lessons were to be assigned. Feeling more confidence in himself, James went about this work in business fashion, and when recess came, the comments made by the pupils in the playground were generally favorable.

"He's going to make a good teacher," said one of the girls, "as good as any we've had, and he's so young too."

"He goes to work as if he knew how," said another. "I didn't think Jimmy Garfield had so much in him."

"Oh, he's smart!" said another. "Just think of brother Ben trying to keep school, and he's just as old as James."

Meanwhile Tom Bassett and Bill Stackpole had a private conference together.

"What do you think of Jim's speech, Bill?" asked Tom.

"Oh, it sounded well enough, but I'll bet he was trembling in his boots all the while he was talkin'."

"Maybe so, but he seemed cool enough."

"Oh, that was all put on. Did you hear what he said about keepin' order?"

"Yes, he kinder looked at you an' me when he was talkin'."

"I guess he heard about our turnin' out the last teacher."

"Of course. I tell you, it took some cheek to come here and order 'round us boys that has known him all his life."

"That's so. Do you think he's goin' to maintain order, as he calls it?"

"You just wait till afternoon. He'll know better then."

James did not go out to recess the first day. He had some things to do affecting the organization of the school, and so he remained at his desk.

Several of the pupils came up to consult him on one point or another, and he received them all with that pleasant manner which throughout his life was characteristic of him. To one and another he gave a hint or a suggestion, based upon his knowledge of their character and abilities. One of the boys said: "Do you think I'd better study grammar, Jimmy—I mean Mr. Garfield?"

James smiled. He knew the slip was unintentional. Of course it would not do for him to allow himself to be addressed in school by a pupil as Jimmy.

"Yes," he answered, "unless you think you know all about it already."

"I don't know the first thing about it."

"Then, of course, you ought to study it. Why shouldn't you?"

"But I can't make nothin' out of it. I can't understand it nohow."

"Then you need somebody to explain it to you."

"It's awful stupid."

"I don't think you will find it so when you come to know more about it. I shall be ready to explain it. I think I can make you understand it."

Another had a sum he could not do. So James found the recess pass quickly away, and again the horde of scholars poured into the school-room.

It was not till afternoon that the conflict came.

Tom Bassett belonged to the first class in geography.

James called out the class.

All came out except Tom, who lounged carelessly in his seat.

"Thomas, don't you belong to this class?" asked the young teacher.

"I reckon I do."

"Then why don't you come out to recite?"

"Oh, I feel lazy," answered Tom, with a significant smile, as if to inquire, "What are you goin' to do about it?"

James thought to himself with a thrill of unpleasant excitement, "It's coming. In ten minutes I shall know whether Tom Bassett or I is to rule this school."

His manner was calm, however, as he said, "That is no excuse. I can't accept it. As your teacher I order you to join your class."

"Can't you wait till to-morrow?" asked Tom, with a grin, which was reflected on the faces of several other pupils.

"I think I understand you," said James, with outward calmness. "You defy my authority."

"You're only a boy like me," said Tom; "I don't see why I should obey you."

"If you were teacher, and I pupil, I should obey you," said James, "and I expect the same of you."

"Oh, go on with the recitation!" said Tom, lazily. "Never mind me!"

James felt that he could afford to wait no longer. Turning to the class, he said, "I shall have to delay you for a minute."

He walked deliberately up to the seat where Tom Bassett was sitting.

Tom squared off in the expectation of an assault; but, with the speed of lightning, the young teacher grasped him by the collar, and, with a strength that surprised himself, dragged him from his seat, in spite of his struggles, till he reached the place where the class was standing.

By this time Bill Stackpole felt called upon to help his partner in rebellion.

"You let him alone!" he said, menacingly, stepping forward.

"One at a time!" said James, coolly. "I will be ready for you in a minute."

He saw that there was only one thing to do.

He dragged Tom to the door, and forcibly ejected him, saying, "When you get ready to obey me you can come back."

He had scarcely turned when Bill Stackpole was upon him.

With a quick motion of the foot James tripped him up, and, still retaining his grasp on his collar, said, "Will you go or stay?"

Bill was less resolute than Tom.

"I guess I'll stay," he said; then picked himself up and resumed his place in the class.

Apparently calm, James returned to his desk, and commenced hearing the class recite.

The next morning, on his way to school, James overtook Tom Bassett, who eyed him with evident embarrassment. Tom's father had sent him back to school, and Tom did not dare disobey.

"Good morning, Tom," said James, pleasantly.

"Mornin'!" muttered Tom.

"I hope you are going to school?"

"Father says I must."

"I am glad of that, too. By the way, Tom, I think I shall have to get some of the scholars to help me with some of the smaller pupils. I should like to get you to hear the lowest class in arithmetic to-day."

"You want me to help you teach?" exclaimed Tom, in amazement.

"Yes; it will give me more time for the higher classes."

"And you don't bear no malice on account of yesterday?"

"Oh, no; we are too good friends to mind such a trifle."

"Then," said Tom, impulsively, "you won't have no more trouble with me. I'll help you all I can."

There was general surprise felt when the young teacher and his rebellious scholar were seen approaching the school-house, evidently on the most friendly terms. There was still greater surprise when, during the forenoon, James requested Tom to hear the class already mentioned. At recess Tom proclaimed his intention to lick any boy that was impudent to the teacher, and the new Garfield administration seemed to be established on a firm basis.

This incident, which is based upon an actual resort to war measures on the part of the young teacher, is given to illustrate the strength as well as the amiability of Garfield's character. It was absolutely necessary that he should show his ability to govern.

CHAPTER XIII.
JAMES LEAVES GEAUGA SEMINARY

While teaching his first school James "boarded round" among the families who sent pupils to his school. It was not so pleasant as having a permanent home, but it afforded him opportunities of reaching and influencing his scholars which otherwise he could not have enjoyed. With his cheerful temperament and genial manners, he could hardly fail to be an acquisition to any family with whom he found a home. He was ready enough to join in making the evenings pass pleasantly, and doubtless he had ways of giving instruction indirectly, and inspiring a love of learning similar to that which he himself possessed.

He returned to school with a small sum of money in his pocket, which was of essential service to him in his economical way of living. But he brought also an experience in imparting knowledge to others which was still greater value.

An eminent teacher has said that we never fully know anything till we have tried to impart it to others.

James remained at the Geauga Seminary for three years. Every winter he taught school, and with success. In one of these winter sessions, we are told by Rev. William M. Thayer, in his biography of Garfield, that he was applied to by an ambitious student to instruct him in geometry. There was one difficulty in the way, and that a formidable one. He was entirely unacquainted with geometry himself. But, he reflected, here is an excellent opportunity for me to acquire a new

branch of knowledge. Accordingly he procured a
text-book, studied it faithfully at night, keeping
sufficiently far ahead of his pupil to qualify him to
be his guide and instructor, and the pupil never
dreamed that his teacher, like himself, was tra-
versing unfamiliar ground.

It was early in his course at Geauga that he
made the acquaintance of one who was to prove
his closest and dearest friend—the young lady
who in after years was to become his wife. Lucretia Rudolph was the daughter of a farmer in
the neighborhood—"a quiet, thoughtful girl, of
singularly sweet and refined disposition, fond of
study and reading, and possessing a warm heart,
and a mind capable of steady growth." Probably
James was first attracted to her by intellectual
sympathy and a community of tastes; but as time
passed he discerned in her something higher and
better than mere intellectual aspiration; and who
shall say in the light that has been thrown by recent events on the character of Lucretia Garfield,
that he was not wholly right?

Though we are anticipating the record, it may
be in place to say here that the acquaintance
formed here was renewed and ripened at Hiram
College, to which in time both transferred themselves. There as pupil-teacher James Garfield became in one branch the instructor of his future
wife, and it was while there that the two became
engaged. It was a long engagement. James had
to wait the traditional "seven years" for his wife,
but the world knows how well he was repaid for
his long waiting.

"Did you know Mrs. Garfield?" asked a reporter of the Chicago *Inter-Ocean* of Mr. Philo Chamberlain, of Cleveland. "Yes, indeed," was the reply:

My wife knows her intimately. They used to teach school together in Cleveland. Mrs. Garfield is a splendid lady. She wasn't what you would call a brilliant teacher, but she was an unusually good one, very industrious, and the children made rapid progress in their studies under her. And then she was studious, too. Why, she acquired three languages while she was in school, both as a student and a teacher, and she spoke them well, I am told. They were married shortly after he came back from Williams, and I forgot to tell you a nice little thing about the time when he paid Dr. Robinson back the money he had spent on him. When Dr. Robinson refused to take the interest, which amounted to a snug little sum, Garfield said: 'Well, Doctor, that is one big point in my favor, as now I can get married.' It seems that they had been engaged for a long time, but had to wait till he could get something to marry on. And I tell you it isn't every young man that will let the payment of a self-imposed debt stand between him and getting married to the girl he loves.

Without anticipating too far events we have not yet reached, it may be said that Lucretia Garfield's education and culture made her not the wife only, but the sympathetic friend and intellectual helper of her husband. Her early studies were of service to her in enabling her partially to prepare for college her two oldest boys. She assisted her husband also in his literary plans, without losing the domestic character of a good wife, and the refining graces of a true woman.

But let us not forget that James is still a boy in his teens. He had many hardships to encounter, and many experiences to go through before he could set up a home of his own. He had studied three years, but his education had only begun. The Geauga Seminary was only an academy, and hardly the equal of the best academies to be found at the East.

He began to feel that he had about exhausted its facilities, and to look higher. He had not far to look.

During the year 1851 the Disciples, the religious body to which young Garfield had attached himself, opened a collegiate school at Hiram, in Portage County, which they called an eclectic school. Now it ranks as a college, but at the time James entered it, it had not assumed so ambitious a title.

It was not far away, and James' attention was naturally drawn to it. There was an advantage also in its location. Hiram was a small country village, where the expenses of living were small, and, as we know, our young student's purse was but scantily filled. Nevertheless, so limited were his means that it was a perplexing problem how he would be able to pay his way.

He consulted his mother, and, as was always the case, found that she sympathized fully in his purpose of obtaining a higher education. Pecuniary help, however, she could not give, nor had he at this time any rich friends upon whom he could call for the pittance he required.

But James was not easily daunted. He had gone to Geauga Seminary with but seventeen dollars in his pocket; he had remained there three years, maintaining himself by work at his old trade of carpenter and teaching, and had graduated owing nothing. He had become self-reliant, and felt that what he had done at Chester he could do at Hiram.

So one fine morning he set out, with a light heart and a pocket equally light, for the infant institution from which he hoped so much.

The Board of Trustees were in session, as we learn from the account given by one of their number, when James arrived and sought an audience.

After a little delay, the doorkeeper was instructed to bring him in.

James was nineteen at this time. He was no longer as homespun in appearance as when he sat upon a log with Dr. Robinson, in the seclusion of the woods, and asked his advice about a career. Nevertheless, he was still awkward. He had grown rapidly, was of slender build, and had no advantages of dress to recommend him. One who saw him in after-life, with his noble, imposing presence, would hardly recognize any similarity between him and the raw country youth who stood awkwardly before the Board of Trustees, to plead his cause. It happens not unfrequently that a lanky youth develops into a fine-looking man. Charles Sumner, at the age of twenty, stood six feet two inches in his stockings, and weighed but one hundred and twenty pounds! Yet in after-life he was a man of noble presence.

But all this while we are leaving James in suspense before the men whose decision is to affect his life so powerfully.

"Well, young man," asked the Principal, "what can we do for you?"

"Gentlemen," said James, earnestly, "I want an education, and would like the privilege of making the fires and sweeping the floors of the building to pay part of my expenses."

There was in his bearing and countenance an earnestness and an intelligence which impressed the members of the board.

"Gentlemen," said Mr. Frederic Williams, one of the trustees, "I think we had better try this young man."

Another member, turning to Garfield, said: "How do we know, young man, that the work will be done as we may desire?"

"Try me," was the answer; "try me two weeks, and if it is not done to your entire satisfaction, I will retire without a word."

"That seems satisfactory," said the member who had asked the question.

"What studies do you wish to pursue?" asked one gentleman.

"I want to prepare for college. I shall wish to study Latin, Greek, mathematics, and anything else that may be needed."

"Have you studied any of these already?"

"Yes, sir."

"Where?"

"At the Geauga Seminary. I can refer you to the teachers there. I have studied under them for three years, and they know all about me."

"What is your name?"

"James A. Garfield."

"There is something in that young man," said one of the trustees to Mr. Williams. "He seems thoroughly in earnest, and I believe will be a hard worker."

"I agree with you," was the reply.

James was informed that his petition was granted, and he at once made arrangements for his residence at Hiram.

CHAPTER XIV.
AT HIRAM INSTITUTE.

Hiram, the seat of the Eclectic Institute, was not a place of any pretension. It was scarcely a village, but rather a hamlet. Yet the advantages which the infant institution offered drew together a considerable number of pupils of both sexes, sons and daughters of the Western Reserve farmers, inspired with a genuine love of learning, and too sensible to waste their time on mere amusement.

This is the account given of it by President B.A. Hinsdale, who for fifteen years has ably presided over its affairs:

The institute building, a plain but substantially built brick structure, was put on the top of a windy hill, in the middle of a cornfield. One of the cannon that General Scott's soldiers dragged to the City of Mexico in 1847, planted on the roof of the new structure, would not have commanded a score of farm houses.

Here the school opened at the time Garfield was closing his studies at Chester. It had been in operation two terms when he offered himself for enrollment. Hiram furnished a location, the Board of Trustees a building and the first teacher, the surrounding country students, but the spiritual Hiram made itself. Everything was new. Society, traditions, the genius of the school, had to be evolved from the forces of the teachers and pupils, limited by the general and local environment. Let no one be surprised when I say that such a school as this was the best of all places for young Garfield. There was freedom, opportunity, a large society of rapidly and eagerly opening young minds, instructors who were learned enough to instruct him, and abundant scope for ability and force of character, of which he had a superabundance.

Few of the students who came to Hiram in that day had more than a district-school education, though some had attended the high schools and academies scattered over the country; so that Garfield, though he had made but slight progress in the classics and the higher mathematics previous to his arrival, ranked well up with the first scholars. In ability, all acknowledged that he was the peer of any; soon his superiority to all others was generally conceded.

So James entered upon his duties as janitor and bell-ringer. It was a humble position for the future President of the United States; but no work is humiliating which is undertaken with a right aim and a useful object. Of one thing my boy-reader may be sure—the duties of the offices were satisfactorily performed. The school-rooms were well cared for, and the bell was rung punctually. This is shown by the fact that, after the two weeks of probation, he was still continued in office, though doubtless in the large number of students of limited means in the institute there was more than one that would have been glad to relieve him of his office.

It will hardly be supposed, however, that the position of janitor and bell-ringer could pay all his expenses. He had two other resources. In term-time he worked at his trade of carpenter as opportunity offered, and in the winter, as at Chester, he sought some country town where he could find employment as a teacher.

The names of the places where he taught are not known to me, though doubtless there is many an Ohio farmer, or mechanic, or, perchance, professional man, who is able to boast that he was partially educated by a President of the United States.

As characteristic of his coolness and firmness,

I am tempted to record an incident which happened to him in one of his winter schools.

There were some scholars about as large as himself, to whom obedience to the rules of the school was not quite easy—who thought, in consideration of their age and size, that they might venture upon acts which would not be tolerated in younger pupils.

The school had commenced one morning, when the young teacher heard angry words and the noise of a struggle in the school-yard, which chanced to be inclosed. The noise attracted the attention of the scholars, and interfered with the attention which the recitation required.

James Garfield stepped quietly outside of the door, and saw two of his oldest and largest pupils engaged in a wrestling match. For convenience we will call them Brown and Jones.

"What are you about, boys?" asked the teacher. The two were so earnestly engaged in their conflict that neither returned an answer.

"This must be stopped immediately," said James, decisively. "It is disrespectful to me, and disturbs the recitations."

He might as well have spoken to the wind. They heard, but they continued their fight.

"This must stop, or I will stop it myself," said the teacher.

The boys were not afraid. Each was about as large as the teacher, and they felt that if he interfered he was likely to get hurt.

James thought he had given sufficient warning. The time had come to act. He stepped quickly forward, seized one of the combatants, and with a sudden exertion of strength, threw him over the fence. Before he had time to recover from his surprise his companion was lifted over in the same manner.

"Now, go on with your fighting if you wish," said the young teacher; "though I advise you to shake hands and make up. When you get through come in and report."

The two young men regarded each other foolishly. Somehow all desire to fight had been taken away.

"I guess we'll go in now," said Brown.

"I'm with you," said Jones, and Garfield entered the school-room, meekly followed by the two refractory pupils. There was not much use in resisting the authority of a teacher who could handle them with such ease.

James did not trouble them with any moral lecture. He was too sensible. He felt that all had been said and done that was required.

But how did he spend his time at the new seminary, and how was he regarded? Fortunately we have the testimony of a lady, now residing in Illinois, who was one of the first students at Hiram. "When he first entered the school," she writes,

He paid for his schooling by doing janitor's work, sweeping the floor and ringing the bell. I can see him even now standing in the morning with his hand on the bell-rope, ready to give the signal, calling teachers and scholars to engage in the duties of the day. As we passed by, entering the school-room, he had a cheerful word for every one. He was probably the most popular person in the institution. He was always good-natured, fond of conversation, and very entertaining. He was witty and quick at repartee, but his jokes, though brilliant and sparkling, were always harmless, and he never would willingly hurt another's feelings.

Afterward he became an assistant teacher, and while pursuing his classical studies, preparatory to his college course, he taught the English branches. He was a most entertaining teacher—ready with illustrations, and possessing in a marked degree the power of exciting the interest of the scholars, and afterward making clear to them the lessons. In the arithmetic class there were ninety pupils, and I can not remember a time when there was any flagging in the interest. There were never any cases of unruly conduct, or a disposition to shirk. With scholars who were slow of comprehension, or to whom recitations were a burden, on account of their modest or retiring dispositions, he was specially attentive, and by encouraging words and gentle assistance would manage to put all at their ease, and awaken in them a confidence in themselves. He was not much given to amusements or the sports of the playground. He was too industrious, and too anxious to make the utmost of his opportunities to study.

He was a constant attendant at the regular meetings for prayer, and his vigorous exhortations and apt remarks upon the Bible lessons were impressive and interesting. There was a cordiality in his disposition which won quickly the favor and esteem of others. He had a happy habit of shaking hands, and would give a hearty grip which betokened a kind-hearted feeling for all. He was always ready to turn his mind and hands in any direction whereby he might add to his meagre store of money.

One of his gifts was that of mezzotint drawing, and he gave instruction in this branch. I was one of his pupils in this, and have now the picture of a cross upon which he did some shading and put on the finishing touches. Upon the margin is written, in the name of the noted teacher, his own name and his pupil's. There are also two other drawings, one of a large European bird on the bough of a tree, and the other a church yard scene in winter, done by him at that time. In those days the faculty and pupils were wont to call him "the second Webster," and the remark was common, "He will fill the White House yet." In the Lyceum he early took rank far above the others as a speaker and debater.

During the month of June the entire school went in carriages to their annual grove meeting at Randolph, some twenty-five miles away. On this trip he was the life of the party, occasionally bursting out in an eloquent strain at the sight of a bird or a trailing vine, or a venerable giant of the forest. He would repeat poetry by the hour, having a very retentive memory.

At the Institute the members were like a band of brothers and sisters, all struggling to advance in knowledge. Then all dressed plainly, and there was no attempt or pretence at dressing fashionably or stylishly. Hiram was a little country place, with no fascinations or worldly attractions to draw off the minds of the students from their work.

Such is an inside view—more graphic than any description I can give—of the life of James Garfield at Hiram Institute.

CHAPTER XV.
THREE BUSY YEARS.

Among the readers of this volume there may be boys who are preparing for college. They will be interested to learn the extent of James Garfield's scholarship, when he left the Geauga Academy, and transferred himself to the Institute at Hiram. Though, in his own language, he remembers with great satisfaction the work which was accomplished for him at Chester, that satisfaction does not spring from the amount that he had acquired, but rather that while there he had formed a definite purpose and plan to complete a college course. For, as the young scholar truly remarks, "It is a great point gained when a young man makes up his mind to devote several years to the accomplishment of a definite work."

When James entered at Hiram, he had studied Latin only six weeks, and just begun Greek.
He was therefore merely on the threshold of his
preparatory course for college. To anticipate a little, he completed this course, and fitted himself
to enter the Junior class at Williams College in
the space of three years. How much labor this
required many of my readers are qualified to understand. It required him to do nearly six years'
work in three, though interrupted by work of
various kinds necessary for his support.

He was not yet able to live luxuriously, or
even, as we suppose, comfortably. He occupied a
room with four other students, which could hardly have been favorable for study. Yet, in the first
term he completed six books of Caesar's commen-
taries, and made good progress in Greek. During
the first winter he taught a school at Warrens-
ville, receiving the highest salary he had yet been
paid, eighteen dollars a month—of course in addition to board.

At the commencement of the second year the
president sent for him.

James obeyed the summons, wondering
whether he was to receive any reprimand for
duty unfulfilled.

President Hayden received him cordially,
thus dissipating his apprehensions.

"Garfield," he said, "Mr. ——, tutor in English
and ancient languages, is sick, and it is doubtful
whether he will be able to resume his duties. Do
you think you can fill his place, besides carrying

on your own work as student?"

Young Garfield's face flushed with pleasure. The compliment was unexpected, but in every way the prospect it opened was an agreeable one. His only doubt was as to his qualifications.

"I should like it very much," he said, "if you think I am qualified."

"I have no doubt on that point. You will teach only what is familiar to you, and I believe you have a special faculty for imparting knowledge."

"Thank you very much, Mr. Hayden," said Garfield. "I will accept with gratitude, and I will do my best to give satisfaction."

How well he discharged his office may be inferred from the testimony given in the last chapter.

Though a part of his time was taken up in teaching others, he did not allow it to delay his own progress. Still before him he kept the bright beacon of a college education. He had put his hand to the plow, and he was not one to turn back or loiter on the way. That term he began Xenophon's Anabasis, and was fortunate enough to find a home in the president's family.

But he was not content with working in termtime. When the summer brought a vacation, he felt that it was too long a time to be lost. He induced ten students to join him, and hired Professor Dunshee to give them lessons for one month. During that time he read the Eclogues and Georgics of Virgil entire, and the first six books of Homer's Iliad, accompanied by a thorough drill in the Latin and Greek grammar. He must have "toiled terribly," and could have had few moments for recreation. When the fall term commenced, in company with Miss Almeda Booth, a mature young lady of remarkable intellect, and some other students, he formed a Translation society, which occupied itself with the Book of Romans, of course in the Greek version. During the succeeding winter he read the whole of "Demosthenes on the Crown."

The mental activity of the young man (he was now twenty) seems exhaustless. All this time he took an active part in a literary society composed of some of his fellow-students. He had already become an easy, fluent, and forcible speaker—a very necessary qualification for the great work of his life.

"Oh, I suppose he had a talent for it," some of my young readers may say.

Probably he had; indeed, it is certain that he had, but it may encourage them to learn that he found difficulties at the start. When a student at Geauga, he made his first public speech. It was a six minutes' oration at the annual exhibition, delivered in connection with a literary society to which he belonged. He records in a diary kept at the time that he "was very much scared," and "very glad of a short curtain across the platform that hid my shaking legs from the audience." Such experiences are not uncommon in the career of men afterward noted for their ease in public speaking. I can recall such, and so doubtless can any man of academic or college training. I wish to impress upon my young reader that Garfield was indebted for what he became to earnest work.

While upon the subject of public speaking I am naturally led to speak of young Garfield's religious associations. His mind has already been impressed with the importance of the religious element, and he felt that no life would be complete without it. He had joined the Church of the Disciples, the same to which his uncle belonged, and was baptized in a little stream that runs into the Chagrin River. The creed of this class of religious believers is one likely to commend itself in most respects to the general company of Christians; but as this volume is designed to steer clear of sect or party, I do not hold any further reference to it necessary. What concerns us more is, that young Garfield, in accordance with the liberal usages of the Disciples, was invited on frequent occasions to officiate as a lay preacher in the absence of the regular pastor of the Church of the Disciples at Hiram.

Though often officiating as a preacher, I do not find that young Garfield ever had the ministry in view. On the other hand, he early formed the design of studying for the legal profession, as he gradually did, being admitted to the bar of Cuyahoga County, in 1860, when himself president of Hiram College.

So passed three busy and happy years. Young Garfield had but few idle moments. In teaching others, in pursuing his own education, in taking part in the work of the literary society, and in Sunday exhortations, his time was well filled up. But neither his religion nor his love of study made him less companionable. He was wonderfully popular. His hearty grasp of the hand, his genial manner, his entire freedom from conceit, his readiness to help others, made him a general favorite. Some young men, calling themselves religious, assume a sanctimonious manner, that repels, but James Garfield never was troubled in this way. He believed that

> Religion never was designed
> To make our pleasures less,

and was always ready to take part in social pleasures, provided they did not interfere with his work.

And all this while, with all his homely surroundings, he had high thoughts for company. He wrote to a student, afterward his own successor to the presidency, words that truly describe his own aspirations and habits of mind:

> Tell me, Burke, do you not feel a spirit stirring within you that longs *to know, to do, and to dare*, to hold converse with the great world of thought, and hold before you some high and noble object to which the vigor of your mind and the strength of your arm may be given? Do you not have longings like these which you breathe to no one, and which you feel must be heeded, or you will pass through life unsatisfied and regretful? I am sure you have them, and they will forever cling round your heart till you obey their mandate.

The time had come when James was ready to take another step upward. The district school had been succeeded by Geauga Seminary, that by Hiram Institute, and now he looked Eastward for still higher educational privileges. There was a college of his own sect at Bethany, not far away, but the young man was not so blinded by this consideration as not to understand that it was not equal to some of the best known colleges at the East.

Which should he select?

He wrote to the presidents of Brown University, Yale, and Williams, stating how far he had advanced, and inquiring how long it would take to complete their course.

From all he received answers, but the one from President Hopkins, of Williams College, ended with the sentence, "If you come here, we shall be glad to do what we can for you." This sentence, so friendly and cordial, decided the young man who otherwise would have found it hard to choose between the three institutions.

"My mind is made up," he said. "I shall start for Williams College next week."

He was influenced also by what he already knew of Dr. Hopkins. He was not a stranger to the high character of his intellect, and his theological reputation. He felt that here was a man of high rank in letters who was prepared to be not only his teacher and guide, but his personal friend, and for this, if for no other reason, he decided in favor of Williams College. To a young man circumstanced as he was, a word of friendly sympathy meant much.

CHAPTER XVI.
ENTERING WILLIAMS COLLEGE.

James Garfield had reached the mature age of twenty-two years when he made his first entrance into Williamstown. He did not come quite empty-handed. He had paid his expenses while at Hiram, and earned three hundred and fifty dollars besides, which he estimated would carry him through the Junior year. He was tall and slender, with a great shock of light hair, rising nearly erect from a broad, high forehead. His face was open, kindly, and thoughtful, and it did not require keen perception of character to discern something above the common in the awkward Western youth, in his decidedly shabby raiment.

Young Garfield would probably have enjoyed the novel sensation of being well dressed, but he had never had the opportunity of knowing how it seemed. That ease and polish of manner which come from mingling in society he entirely lacked. He was as yet a rough diamond, but a diamond for all that.

Among his classmates were men from the cities, who stared in undisguised amazement at the tall, lanky young man who knocked at the doors of the college for admission.

"Who is that rough-looking fellow?" asked a member of a lower class, pointing out Garfield, as he was crossing the college campus.

"Oh, that is Garfield; he comes from the Western Reserve."

"I suppose his clothes were made by a Western Reserve tailor."

"Probably," answered his classmate, smiling.

"He looks like a confirmed rustic."

"That is true, but there is something in him. I am in his division, and I can tell you that he has plenty of talent."

"His head is big enough."

"Yes, he has a large brain—a sort of Websterian intellect. He is bound to be heard of."

"It is a pity he is so awkward."

"Oh, that will wear off. He has a hearty, cordial way with him, and though at first we were disposed to laugh at him, we begin to like him."

"He's as old as the hills. At any rate, he looks so."

"How old are you?"

"Seventeen."

"Compared with you he is, for he is nearly twenty-three. However, it is never too late to learn. He is not only a good scholar, but he is very athletic, and there are few in college who can equal him in athletic sports."

"Why didn't he come to college before? What made him wait till he was an old man?"

"I understand that he has had a hard struggle with poverty. All the money he has he earned by hard labor. Dr. Hopkins seems to have taken a liking to him. I saw him walking with the doctor the other day."

This conversation describes pretty accurately the impression made by Garfield upon his classmates, and by those in other classes who became acquainted with him. At first they were disposed to laugh at the tall, awkward young man and his manners, but soon his real ability, and his cordial, social ways won upon all, and he was installed as a favorite. The boys began to call him Old Gar, and regarded him with friendship and increasing respect, as he grew and developed intellectually, and they began to see what manner of man he was.

Perhaps the readiest way for a collegian to make an impression upon his associates is to show a decided talent for oratory. They soon discovered at Williams that Garfield had peculiar gifts in this way. His speaking at clubs, and before the church of his communion in Hiram, had been for him a valuable training. He joined a society, and soon had an opportunity of showing that he was a ready and forcible speaker.

One day there came startling news to the college. Charles Sumner had been struck down in the Senate chamber by Preston S. Brooks, of South Carolina, for words spoken in debate. The hearts of the students throbbed with indignation—none more fiercely than young Garfield's. At an indignation meeting convened by the students he rose and delivered, so says one who heard him, "one of the most impassioned and eloquent speeches ever delivered in old Williams."

It made a sensation.

"Did you hear Old Gar's speech at the meeting?" asked one of another.

"No, I did not get in in time."

"It was great. I never heard him speak better. Do you know what I think?"

"Well?"

"Gar will be in Congress some day himself. He has rare powers of debate, and is a born orator."

"I shouldn't wonder myself if you were right. If he ever reaches Congress he will do credit to old Williams."

James had given up his trade as a carpenter. He was no longer obliged to resort to it, or, at any rate, he preferred to earn money in a different way. So one winter he taught penmanship at North Pownal, in Vermont, a post for which he was qualified, for he had a strong, bold, handsome hand.

"Did you know Mr. Arthur, who taught school here last winter?" asked one of his writing pupils of young Garfield.

"No; he was not a student of Williams."

"He graduated at Union College, I believe."

"Was he a good teacher?"

"Yes, he was very successful, keeping order without any trouble, though the school is considered a hard one."

This was Chester A. Arthur, whose name in after years was to be associated with that of the writing-teacher, who was occupying the same room as his Presidential successor. But to James Garfield, at that time, the name meant nothing, and it never occurred to him what high plans Providence had for them both. It was one of those remarkable cases in which the paths of two men who are joined in destiny traverse each other. Was it not strange that two future occupants of the Presidential chair should be found teaching in the same school-room, in an obscure Vermont village, two successive winters?

As the reader, though this is the biography of Garfield, may feel a curiosity to learn what sort of a teacher Arthur was, I shall, without apology, conclude this chapter with the story of a pupil of his who, in the year 1853, attended the district school at Cohoes, then taught by Chester A. Arthur. I find it in the Troy *Times*:

In the year 1853 the writer attended the district school at Cohoes. The high department did not enjoy a very enviable reputation for being possessed of that respect due from the pupils to teacher. During the year there had been at least four teachers in that department, the last one only remaining one week. The Board of Education had found it difficult to obtain a pedagogue to take charge of the school, until a young man, slender as a May-pole and six feet high in his stockings, applied for the place. He was engaged at once, although he was previously informed of the kind of timber he would be obliged to hew.

Promptly at nine o'clock A.M. every scholar was on hand to welcome the man who had said that he would "conquer the school or forfeit his reputation." Having called the morning session to order, he said that he had been engaged to take charge of the school. He came with his mind prejudiced against the place. He had heard of the treatment of the former teachers by the pupils, yet he was not at all embarrassed, for he felt that, with the prop-

er recognition of each other's rights, teacher
and scholars could live together in harmony.
He did not intend to threaten, but he intended
to make the scholars obey him, and would try
and win the good-will of all present. He had
been engaged to take charge of that room, and
he wished the co-operation of every pupil in
so doing. He had no club, ruler, or whip, but
appealed directly to the hearts of every young
man and young lady in the room. Whatever he
should do, he would at least show to the people of this place that this school could be gov-
erned. He spoke thus and feelingly at times,
yet with perfect dignity he displayed that executive ability which in after years made him
such a prominent man. Of course the people,
especially the boys, had heard fine words spoken before, and at once a little smile seemed
to flit across the faces of the leading spirits in
past rebellions.

The work of the forenoon began, when a
lad of sixteen placed a marble between his
thumb and finger, and, with a snap, sent it rolling across the floor. As the tall and handsome
teacher saw this act, he arose from his seat,
and, without a word, walked toward the lad.

"Get up, sir," he said.

The lad looked at him to see if he was in
earnest; then he cast his eyes toward the large
boys to see if they were not going to take up
his defense.

"Get up, sir," said the teacher a second
time, and he took him by the collar of his jack-

et as if to raise him. The lad saw he had no common man to deal with, and he rose from his seat.

"Follow me, sir," calmly spoke the teacher, and he led the way toward the hall, while the boy began to tremble, wondering if the new teacher was going to take him out and kill him. The primary department was presided over by a sister of the new teacher, and into this room he led the young transgressor.

Turning to his sister he said: "I have a pupil for you; select a seat for him, and let him remain here. If he makes any disturbance whatever, inform me." Turning to the boy he said: "Young man, mind your teacher, and do not leave your seat until I give permission," and he was gone.

The lad sat there, feeling very sheepish, and as misery loves company, it was not long before he was gratified to see the door open and observe his seat-mate enter with the new teacher, who repeated the previous orders, when he quietly and with dignity withdrew.

The number was subsequently increased to three, the teacher returning each time without a word to the other scholars concerning the disposition made of the refractory lads. The effect upon the rest of the school was remarkable. As no intimation of the disposition of the boys was given, not a shade of anger displayed on the countenance of the new teacher, nor any appearances of blood were noticeable upon his hands, speculation was rife as to what he had done with the three chaps. He spoke kindly to all, smiled upon the scholars who did well in their classes, and seemed to inspire all present with the truth of his remarks uttered at the opening of the session.

At recess the mystery that had enveloped the school was cleared away, for the three lads in the primary department were seen as the rest of the scholars filed by the door. While all the rest enjoyed the recess, the three lads were obliged to remain in their seats, and when school was dismissed for the forenoon, the new teacher entered the primary-room, and was alone with the young offenders. He sat down by them, and like a father talked kindly and gave good advice. No parent ever used more fitting words nor more impressed his offspring with the fitness thereof than did the new teacher. Dismissing them, he told them to go home, and when they returned to school to be good boys.

That afternoon the boys were in their seats, and in two weeks' time there was not a scholar in the room who would not do anything the teacher asked. He was beloved by all, and his quiet manner and cool, dignified ways made him a great favorite. He only taught two terms, and every reasonable inducement was offered to prevail upon him to remain, but without avail. His reply was: "I have accomplished all I intended, namely, conquered what you thought was a wild lot of boys, and received the discipline that I required. I regret leaving my charge, for I have learned to love them, but I am to enter a law office at once."

That teacher was Chester A. Arthur, now President of the United States; the teacher of the primary department was his sister, now Mrs. Haynesworth, and the first of the three refractory boys was the writer. When it was announced that our beloved teacher was to leave us, many tears were shed by his scholars, and as a slight token of our love, we presented him with an elegant volume of poems.

CHAPTER XVII.
LIFE IN COLLEGE.

Probably young Garfield never passed two happier or more profitable years than at Williams College. The Seminaries he had hitherto attended were respectable, but in the nature of things they could not afford the facilities which he now enjoyed. Despite his years of study and struggle there were many things in which he was wholly deficient. He had studied Latin, Greek, and mathematics, but of English literature he knew but little. He had never had time to read for recreation, or for that higher culture which is not to be learned in the class-room.

In the library of Williams College he made his first acquaintance with Shakespeare, and we can understand what a revelation his works must have been to the aspiring youth. He had abstained from reading fiction, doubting whether it was

profitable, since the early days when with a thrill
of boyish excitement he read *Sinbad the Sailor*
and Marryatt's novels. After a while his views as
to the utility of fiction changed. He found that his
mind was suffering from the solid food to which it
was restricted, and he began to make incursions
into the realm of poetry and fiction with excellent
results. He usually limited this kind of reading,
and did not neglect for the fascination of romance
those more solid works which should form the
staple of a young man's reading.

It is well known that among poets Tennyson
was his favorite, so that in after years, when at
fifteen minutes' notice, on the first anniversary
of Lincoln's assassination, he was called upon to
move an adjournment of the House, as a mark of
respect to the martyred President, he was able
from memory to quote in his brief speech, as applicable to Lincoln, the poet's description of some

> Divinely gifted man,
> Whose life in low estate began,
> And on a simple village green,
>   Who breaks his birth's invidious bars,
> And grasped the skirts of happy chance,
> And breasts the blows of circumstance,
>   And grapples with his evil stars;
> Who makes by force his merit known,
> And lives to clutch the golden keys
>   To mould a mighty state's decrees,
> And shape the whisper of the throne;
> And moving up from high to higher,
>   Becomes on Fortune's crowning slope

The pillar of a people's hope,
The center of a world's desire.

I am only repeating the remark made by many when I call attention to the fitness of this description to Garfield himself.

Our young student was fortunate in possessing a most retentive memory. What he liked, especially in the works of his favorite poet, was so impressed upon his memory that he could recite extracts by the hour. This will enable the reader to understand how thoroughly he studied, and how readily he mastered, those branches of knowledge to which his attention was drawn. When in after years in Congress some great public question came up, which required hard study, it was the custom of his party friends to leave Garfield to study it, with the knowledge that in due time he would be ready with a luminous exposition which would supply to them the place of individual study.

Young Garfield was anxious to learn the language of Goethe and Schiller, and embraced the opportunity afforded at college to enter upon the study of German. He was not content with a mere smattering, but learned it well enough to converse in it as well as to read it.

So most profitably the Junior year was spent, but unhappily James had spent all the money which he had brought with him. Should he leave college to earn more? Fortunately, this was not necessary. Thomas Garfield, always unselfishly devoted to the family, hoped to supply his younger brother with the necessary sum, in installments; but proving unable, his old friend, Dr. Robinson, came to his assistance.

"You can pay me when you are able, James," he said.

"If I live I will pay you, doctor. If I do not—"

He paused, for an idea struck him.

"I will insure my life for eight hundred dollars," he continued, "and place the policy in your hands. Then, whether I live or die, you will be secure."

"I do not require this, James," said the doctor kindly.

"Then I feel all the more under obligations to secure you in return for your generous confidence."

It was a sensible and business-like proposal, and the doctor assented. The strong, vigorous young man had no difficulty in securing a policy from a reputable company, and went back to college at the commencement of the Senior year. I wish to add that the young man scrupulously repaid the good doctor's timely loan, for had he failed to do so, I could not have held him up to my young readers as in all respects a model.

There was published at Williams College, in Garfield's time, a magazine called the *Williams Quarterly*. To this the young man became a frequent contributor. In Gen. James S. Brisbin's campaign Life of Garfield, I find three of his poetic contributions quoted, two of which I will also transfer to my pages, as likely to possess some interest for my young reader. The first is called

THE CHARGE OF THE TIGHT BRIGADE,

and commences thus:

Bottles to right of them,
Bottles to left of them,
Bottles in front of them,
    Fizzled and sundered;
Ent'ring with shout and yell,
Boldly they drank and well,
They caught the Tartar then;
Oh, what a perfect sell!
    Sold—the half hundred!
Grinned all the dentals bare,
Swung all their caps in air,
Uncorking bottles there,
Watching the Freshmen, while
    Every one wondered;
Plunged in tobacco smoke,
With many a desperate stroke,
Dozens of bottles broke;
Then they came back, but not,
    Not the half hundred!

Lest from this merry squib, which doubtless celebrated some college prank, wrong conclusions should be drawn, I hasten to say that in college James Garfield neither drank nor smoked.

The next poem is rather long, but it possesses interest as a serious production of one whose name has become a household word. It is entitled

MEMORY.

'Tis beauteous night; the stars look brightly down
Upon the earth, decked in her robe of snow.
No light gleams at the window save my own,
Which gives its cheer to midnight and to me.
And now with noiseless step sweet Memory comes,
And leads me gently through her twilight realms.
What poet's tuneful lyre has ever sung,
Or delicatest pencil e'er portrayed
The enchanted, shadowy land where Memory dwells?
It has its valleys, cheerless, lone, and drear,
Dark-shaded by the lonely cypress tree.
And yet its sunlit mountain tops are bathed
In heaven's own blue. Upon its craggy cliffs,
Robed in the dreamy light of distant years,
Are clustered joys serene of other days;
Upon its gently sloping hillside's bank
The weeping-willows o'er the sacred dust
Of dear departed ones; and yet in that land,
Where'er our footsteps fall upon the shore,
They that were sleeping rise from out the dust
Of death's long, silent years, and round us stand,
As erst they did before the prison tomb
Received their clay within its voiceless halls.

The heavens that bend above that land are hung
With clouds of various hues; some dark and chill,
Surcharged with sorrow, cast their sombre shade
Upon the sunny, joyous land below;
Others are floating through the dreamy air,
White as the falling snow, their margins tinged
With gold and crimson hues; their shadows fall
Upon the flowery meads and sunny slopes,

Soft as the shadows of an angel's wing.
When the rough battle of the day is done,
And evening's peace falls gently on the heart,
I bound away across the noisy years,
Unto the utmost verge of Memory's land,
Where earth and sky in dreamy distance meet,
And Memory dim with dark oblivion joins;
Where woke the first remembered sounds that fell
Upon the ear in childhood's early morn;
And wandering thence along the rolling years,
I see the shadow of my former self
Gliding from childhood up to man's estate.
The path of youth winds down through many a vale,
And on the brink of many a dread abyss,
From out whose darkness comes no ray of light,
Save that a phantom dances o'er the gulf,
And beckons toward the verge. Again, the path
Leads o'er a summit where the sunbeams fall;
And thus, in light and shade, sunshine and gloom,
Sorrow and joy, this life-path leads along.

During the year 1856 young Garfield was one of the editors of the college magazine, from which the above extracts are made. The hours spent upon his contributions to its pages were doubtless well spent. Here, to use his own words, he learned "to hurl the lance and wield the sword and thus prepare for the conflict of life." More than one whose names have since become conspicuous contributed to it while under his charge. Among these were Professor Chadbourne, S.G.W. Benjamin, Horace E. Scudder, W.R. Dimmock, and John Savary. The last-named, now resident in

Washington, has printed, since his old friend's death, a series of sonnets, from which I quote one:

> How many and how great concerns of state
> Lie at the mercy of the meanest things!
> This man, the peer of presidents and kings;
> Nay, first among them, passed through danger's gate
> In war unscathed, and perils out of date,
> To meet a fool whose pistol-shot yet rings
> Around the world, and at mere greatness flings
> The cruel sneer of destiny or fate!
> Yet hath he made the fool fanatic foil
> To valor, patience, nobleness, and wit!
> Nor had the world known, but because of it,
> What virtues grow in suffering's sacred soil.
> The shot which opened like a crack of hell,
> Made all hearts stream with sacred pity's well
> And showed that unity in which we dwell.

CHAPTER XVIII.
THE CANAL-BOY BECOMES
A COLLEGE PRESIDENT.

During his second winter vacation a great temptation assailed James. It was not a temptation to do wrong. That he could easily have resisted.

I must explain.

At Prestenkill, a country village six miles from Troy, N.Y., the young student organized a writing school, to help defray his expenses. Having occasion to visit Troy, his interest in education led him to form an acquaintance with some of the teachers and directors of the public schools.

One of these gentlemen, while walking with him over the sloping sides of a hill overlooking the city, said: "Mr. Garfield, I have a proposition to make to you."

The student listened with interest.

"There is a vacancy in one of our public schools. We want an experienced teacher, and I am sure you will suit us. I offer you the place, with a salary of twelve hundred dollars a year. What do you say?"

The young man's heart beat for a moment with repressible excitement. It was a strong temptation. He was offered, deducting vacations, about one hundred and twenty-five dollars a month, while heretofore his highest wages had been but eighteen dollars per month and board. Moreover, he could marry at once the young lady to whom he had been for years engaged.

He considered the offer a moment, and this was his answer:

"You are not Satan and I am not Jesus, but we are upon the mountain, and you have tempted me powerfully. I think I must say, 'Get thee behind me!' I am poor, and the salary would soon pay my debts and place me in a position of independence; but there are two objections. I could not accomplish my resolution to complete a college course, and should be crippled intellectually for life. Then, my roots are all fixed in Ohio, where people know me and I know them, and this transplanting might not succeed as well in the long run as to go back home and work for smaller pay."

So the young man decided adversely, and it

looks as if his decision was a wise one. It is interesting to conjecture what would have been his
future position had he left college and accepted
the school then offered him. He might still have
been a teacher, well known and of high repute,
but of fame merely local, and without a thought
of the brilliant destiny he had foregone.

So he went back to college, and in the summer of 1856 he graduated, carrying off the highest honor—the metaphysical oration. His class
was a brilliant one. Three became general officers during the rebellion—Garfield, Daviess, and
Thompson. Rockwell's name is well known in official circles; Gilfillan is Treasurer of the United
States. There are others who fill prominent positions. In the class above him was the late Hon.
Phineas W. Hitchcock, who for six years represented Nebraska in the United States Senate—
like Garfield, the architect of his own fortunes.

"What are your plans, Garfield?" asked a
classmate but a short time before graduation.

"I am going back to Ohio, to teach in the school
where I prepared for college."

"What is the name of the school?"

"Hiram Institute."

"I never heard of it."

"It has only a local reputation."

"Will you get a high salary?"

"No; the institute is poor, and can pay me but
little."

"I think you are making a mistake."

"Why so?"

"You are our best scholar, and no one can rival

you in speaking in the societies. You should study law, and then go to one of our large cities and build up a reputation, instead of burying yourself in an out-of-the-way Ohio town, where you may live and die without the world hearing of you."

"Thank you for your good opinion of me. I am not sure whether I deserve it, but if I do, I shall come to the surface some day. Meanwhile, to this humble school (it was not yet a college) I owe a large debt of gratitude. I am under a promise to go back and do what I can to pay that debt."

"In doing so you may sacrifice your own prospects."

"I hope not. At any rate, my mind is made up."

"Oh, well, in that case I will say no more. I know that if your mind is made up, you are bound to go. Only, years hence you will think of my warning."

"At any rate," said Garfield, cordially, "I shall bear in mind the interest you have shown in me. You may be right—I admit that—but I feel that it is my duty to go."

I doubt whether any man of great powers can permanently bury himself, no matter how obscure the position which he chooses. Sooner or later the world will find him out, and he will be lifted to his rightful place. When General Grant occupied a desk in the office of a lawyer in St. Louis, and made a precarious living by collecting bills, it didn't look as if Fame had a niche for him; but occasion came, and lifted him to distinction. So I must confess that the young graduate seemed to be making a mistake when, turning his back upon Williams College, he sought the humble institution where he had taught, as a pupil-teacher, two years before, and occupied a place as instructor, with an humble salary. But even here there was promotion for him. A year later, at the age of twenty-six, he was made president of the institution. It was not, perhaps, a lofty position, for though Hiram Institute now became Hiram College, it was not a college in the New England sense, but rather a superior academy.

Let us pause a minute and see what changes have taken place in ten years.

At the age of sixteen Jimmy Garfield was glad to get a chance to drive a couple of mules on the tow-path of the Ohio and Pennsylvania Canal. The ragged, homespun boy had disappeared. In his place we find James A. Garfield, A.B., president of a Western college—a man of education and culture. And how has this change been brought about! By energy, perseverance, and a resolute purpose—a soul that poverty could not daunt, an ambition which shrank from no hardship, and no amount of labor. They have been years of toil, for it takes time to transform a raw and ignorant country lad into a college president; but the toil has not harmed him—the poverty has not cramped him, nor crippled his energies. "Poverty is very inconvenient," he said on one occasion, in speaking of those early years, "but it is a fine spur to activity, and may be made a rich blessing."

The young man now had an assured income; not a large one, but Hiram was but an humble village. No fashionable people lived there. The people were plain in their tastes, and he could live as well as the best without difficulty. He was employed in a way that interested and pleased him, and but one thing seemed wanting. His heart had never swerved from the young lady with whom he first became acquainted at Geauga, to whom he was more closely drawn at Hiram, and to whom now for some years he had been betrothed. He felt that he could now afford to be married; and so Lucretia Rudolph became Mrs. Garfield—a name loved and honored, for her sake as well as his, throughout the length and breadth of our land. She, too, had been busily and usefully employed in these intervening years. As Mr. Philo Chamberlain, of Cleveland, has told us elsewhere, she has been a useful and efficient teacher in one of the public schools of that city. She has not been content with instructing others, but in her hours of leisure has pursued a private course of study, by which her mind has been broadened and deepened. If some prophetic instinct had acquainted her with the high position which the future had in store for her, she could have taken no fitter course to prepare herself to fulfil with credit the duties which, twenty years after, were to devolve upon her as the wife of the Chief Magistrate of the Union.

This was the wife that Garfield selected, and he found her indeed a helper and a sympathizer in all his sorrows and joys. She has proved equal to any position to which the rising fame of her husband lifted her. Less than a year ago her hus-

band said of her: "I have been wonderfully blessed in the discretion of my wife. She is one of the
coolest and best-balanced women I ever saw. She
is unstampedable. There has not been one soli-
tary instance in my public career when I suffered
in the smallest degree for any remark she ever
made. It would have been perfectly natural for a
woman often to say something that could be mis-
interpreted; but, without any design, and with
the intelligence and coolness of her character,
she has never made the slightest mistake that I
ever heard of. With the competition that has been
against me, such discretion has been a real blessing."

Public men who have risen from humble beginnings often suffer from the mistakes of wives
who have remained stationary, and are unfitted
to sympathize with them in the larger life of their
husbands. But as James A. Garfield grew in the
public esteem, and honors crowded upon him,
step by step his wife kept pace with him, and was
at all times a fitting and sympathetic companion
and helpmeet.

They commenced housekeeping in a neat little
cottage fronting the college campus; and so their
wedded life began. It was a modest home, but a
happy one, and doubtless both enjoyed more happy hours than in the White House, even had the
last sorrowful tragedy never been enacted. As
President, James A. Garfield belonged to the nation; as the head of Hiram College, to his family.
Greatness has its penalties, and a low estate its
compensations.

CHAPTER XIX.
GARFIELD AS A COLLEGE PRESIDENT.

When James Garfield presented himself at Hiram, an awkward, overgrown boy of nineteen, in his rustic garb, and humbly asked for the position of janitor and bell-ringer, suppose the trustees had been told, "In seven years your institute will have developed into a college, and that boy will be the president," we can imagine their amazement.

Yet it had all come true. Nowhere, perhaps, but in America could such a thing have happened, and even here it seldom happens that such an upward stride is made in so short a time.

After all, however, the important question to consider is, "What sort of a college president did this humble canal-boy, who counted it promotion when he was elected a janitor and bell-ringer, become?"

For information upon this point, we go to one of his pupils, Rev. I.L. Darsie, of Danbury, Conn., who writes as follows:

I attended the Western Reserve Institute when Garfield was principal, and I recall vividly his method of teaching. He took very kindly to me, and assisted me in various ways, because I was poor, and was janitor of the buildings, and swept them out in the morning and built the fires, as he had done only six years before, when he was a pupil in the same college. He was full of animal spirits, and used to run out on the green every day and play cricket with his scholars. He was a tall, strong man, but dreadfully awkward. Every now and then he would get a hit, and he muffed his ball and lost his hat as a regular thing.* He was left-handed, too, and that made him seem all the clumsier. But he was most powerful and very quick, and it was easy for us to understand how it was that he had acquired the reputation of whipping all the other mule-drivers on the canal, and of making himself the hero of that thoroughfare, when he followed its tow-path, only ten years earlier.

No matter how old the pupils were, Garfield always called us by our first names, and kept himself on the most intimate terms with all. He played with us freely, and we treated him out of the class-room just about as we did one another. Yet he was a most strict disciplinarian, and enforced the rules like a martinet. He combined an affectionate and confiding manner with respect for order in a most successful manner. If he wanted to speak to a pupil, either for reproof or approbation, he would generally manage to get one arm around him, and draw him close up to him. He had a peculiar way of shaking hands, too, giving a twist to your arm, and drawing you right up to him. This sympathetic manner has

* I have seen it somewhere stated that when a Congressman at Washington he retained his interest in the game of base-ball, and always was in attendance when it was possible, at a game between two professional clubs.

helped him to advancement. When I was janitor, he used sometimes to stop me, and ask my opinion about this and that, as if seriously advising with me. I can see now that my opinion could not have been of any value, and that he probably asked me partly to increase my self-respect and partly to show that he felt an interest in me. I certainly was his friend all the firmer for it.

I remember once asking him what was the best way to pursue a certain study.

"Use several text-books," he answered. "Get the views of different authors as you advance. In that way you can plow a deeper furrow. I always study in that way."

He tried hard to teach us to observe carefully and accurately. He broke out one day in the midst of a lesson with, "Henry, how many posts are there under the building downstairs?" Henry expressed his opinion, and the question went around the class, hardly any one getting it right. Then it was, "How many boot-scrapers are there at the door?" "How many windows in the building?" "How many trees in the field?" He was the keenest observer I ever saw. I think he noticed and numbered every button on our coats. A friend of mine was walking with him through Cleveland one day, when Garfield stopped and darted down a cellar-way, asking his companion to follow, and briefly pausing to explain himself. The sign, "Saws and Files," was over the door, and in the depths was heard a regular clicking sound. "I think this fellow is cutting files," said he, "and I have never seen a file cut."

Down they went, and, sure enough, there was a man recutting an old file; and they stayed ten minutes, and found out all about the process. Garfield would never go by anything without understanding it.

Mr. Garfield was very fond of lecturing in the school. He spoke two or three times a week, on all manner of topics, generally scientific, though sometimes literary or historical. He spoke with great freedom, never writing out what he had to say, and I now think that his lectures were a rapid compilation of his current reading, and that he threw it into this form partly for the purpose of impressing it upon his own mind.

His facility of speech was learned when he was a pupil at Hiram. The societies had a rule that every student should take his stand on the platform and speak for five minutes on any topic suggested at the moment by the audience. It was a very trying ordeal. Garfield broke down badly the first two times he tried to speak, but persisted, and was at last, when he went to Williams, one of the best of the five-minute speakers. When he returned as principal, his readiness was striking and remarkable.

Henry James says: "Garfield taught me more than any other man, living or dead, and, proud as I am of his record as a soldier and a statesman, I can hardly forgive him for abandoning the academy and the forum."

So President Hinsdale, one of Garfield's pupils, and his successor as president, testifies:

My real acquaintance with Garfield did not begin till the fall of 1856, when he returned from Williams College. He then found me out, drew near to me, and entered into all my troubles and difficulties pertaining to questions of the future. In a greater or less degree this was true of his relations to his pupils generally. There are hundreds of these men and women scattered over the world to-day, who can not find language strong enough to express their feeling in contemplating Garfield as their old instructor, adviser, and friend.

Since 1856 my relations with him have been as close and confidential as they could be with any man, and much closer and more confidential than they have been with any other man. I do not say that it would be possible for me to know anybody better than I know him, and I know that he possesses all the great elements of character in an extraordinary degree. His interest in humanity has always been as broad as humanity itself, while his lively interest in young men and women, especially if they were struggling in narrow circumstances to obtain an education, is a characteristic known as widely over the world as the footsteps of Hiram boys and girls have wandered.

The help that he furnished hundreds in the

way of suggestions, teaching, encouragement, inspiration, and stimulus was most valuable. His power over students was not so much that of a drill-master, or disciplinarian, as that of one who was able to inspire and energize young people by his own intellectual and moral force.

An illustration of the interest he felt in his pupils may be given.

A student came to the president's study at the close of a college term to bid him good-bye. After the good-bye was said, he lingered, and Garfield said: "I suppose you will be back again in the fall, Henry?"

"No," he stammered, "I am not coming back to Hiram any more. Father says I have got education enough, and that he needs me to work on the farm; that education doesn't help a farmer along any."

He was a bright boy—not a prodigy, by any means, but one of those strong, awkward, large-headed fellows, such as James Garfield had himself been.

"Is your father here?" asked the young president, affected by the boy's evident sorrow.

"Yes, father is here, and is taking my things home for good."

"Well, don't feel badly. Please tell him Mr. Garfield would like to see him at his study before he leaves the college."

"Yes, sir, I will."

In half an hour the father, a sturdy farmer, entered the study and awkwardly sat down.

"So you have come to take Henry home, have you?" asked the president.

"Yes," answered the farmer.

"I sent for you because I wanted to have a little talk with you about Henry's future. He is coming back again in the fall, I hope?"

"Wal, I think not. I don't reckon I can afford to send him any more. He's got eddication enough for a farmer already, and I notice that when they git too much, they sorter git lazy. Yer eddicated farmers are humbugs. Henry's got so far 'long now that he'd rather have his head in a book than be workin'. He don't take no interest in the stock, nor in the farm improvements. Everybody else is dependent in this world on the farmer, and I think that we've got too many eddicated fellows settin' 'round now for the farmers to support."

To this Garfield answered that he was sorry for the father's decision, since his son, if permitted to come the next term, would be far enough advanced to teach school, and so begin to help himself along. Teaching would pay better than working on the farm in the winter.

"Do you really think Henry can teach next winter?" asked the father, to whom the idea was a new one.

"I should think so, certainly," answered Garfield. "But if he can not do so then, he can in a short time."

"Wal, I will think on it. He wants to come back bad enough, and I guess I'll have to let him. I never thought of it that way afore."

The victory was won. Henry came back the next term, and after finishing at Hiram, graduated at an Eastern college.

CHAPTER XX.
GARFIELD BECOMES A STATE SENATOR.

Probably Garfield considered now that he was settled in life. He had married the woman of his choice, set up a pleasant home, and was fully occupied with a class of duties that suited him. Living frugally, he was able to lay by a portion of his salary annually, and saw the way open, if life and health continued, to a moderate prosperity. He seemed to be a born teacher, and his life seemed likely to be passed in that pleasant and tranquil office.

Many years before, while still unmarried, his mother had been a teacher, and one of her experiences when so occupied was so remarkable that I can not forbear quoting it:

About the year 1820 she and her sister were left alone in the world, without provision, so far as the inheritance or possession of property was concerned. Preferring to live among relatives, one went to reside with an uncle in Northern Ohio, and the other, Eliza, afterward Mrs. Garfield, came to another uncle, the father of Samuel Arnold, who then lived on a farm near Norwich, Muskingum County, Ohio. There Eliza Ballou made her home, cheerfully helping at the house or in the field, as was then sometimes the custom in a pioneer country. Having something more than what at that day was an ordinary education, Eliza procured about twenty pupils, and taught a summer school.

The school-house was one of the most primitive kind, and stood in the edge of dense and heavily-timbered woods. One day there came up a fearful storm of wind and rain, accompanied by thunder and lightning. The woods were badly wrecked, but the wind left the old log-house uninjured. Not so the lightning. A bolt struck a tree that projected closely over the roof, and then the roof itself. Some of the pupils were greatly alarmed, and no doubt thought it the crack of doom, or the day of judgment. The teacher, as calm and collected as possible, tried to quiet her pupils and keep them in their places. A man who was one of the pupils, in speaking of the occurrence, says that for a little while he remembered nothing, and then he looked around, and saw, as he thought, the teacher and pupils lying dead on the, floor. Presently the teacher began to move a little. Then, one by one, the pupils got up, with a single exception. Help, medical and otherwise, was obtained as soon as possible for this one, but, though life was saved for a time, reason had forever fled.

This was certainly a fearful experience for a young teacher.

It was while on a visit to her sister, already married, in Northern Ohio, that Eliza made the acquaintance of Abram Garfield, the father of the future President. In this neighborhood, while on a visit to his relatives, at the age of seventeen, James obtained a school and taught for a single term.

Having retraced our steps to record this early experience of James' mother, we take the opportunity to mention an incident in the life of her son, which was omitted in the proper place. The story was told by Garfield himself during his last sickness to Mr. Crump, steward of the White House.

"When I was a youngster," said the President, "and started for college at Hiram, I had just fifteen dollars—a ten-dollar bill in an old, black-leather pocketbook, which was in the breast pocket of my coat, and the other five dollars was in my trowsers' pocket. I was walking along the road, and, as the day was hot, I took off my coat and carried it on my arm, taking good care to feel every moment or two of the pocketbook, for the hard-earned fifteen dollars was to pay my entrance at the college.

"After a while I got to thinking over what college life would be like, and forgot all about the pocketbook for some time, and when I looked again it was gone! I went back mournfully along the road, hunting on both sides for the pocketbook. Presently I came to a house where a young man was leaning over a gate, and he asked me when I came up what I was hunting for. Upon my explaining my loss, and describing the pocketbook, the young man handed it over. That young man," the President added, turning to his devot-

ed physician, "was Dr. Bliss. He saved me for college."

"Yes," said the doctor, "and if I hadn't found
your ten dollars you wouldn't have become President of the United States."

Many a true word is spoken in jest. It might
have happened that the boy would have been so
depressed by the loss of his money that he would
have given up his plan of going to Hiram and returned home to fill an humbler place in the world.

But it is time to return from this digression
and resume our narrative.

Devoted to his profession, young Garfield had
given but little attention to politics. But in the
political campaign of 1857 and 1858 he became interested in the exciting political questions which
agitated the community, and, taking the stump,
he soon acquired the reputation of a forcible and
logical stump orator. This drew the attention of
the voters to him, and in 1859 he was tendered
a nomination to the Ohio Senate from the counties of Portage and Summit. His speeches during
the campaign of that year are said to have been
warm, fresh, and impassioned, and he was elected
by a handsome majority.

This was the first entrance of the future President upon public life. The session was not long,
and the absence of a few weeks at Columbus did
not seriously interfere with his college duties.

In the Senate he at once took high rank. He
was always ready to speak, his past experience
having made this easy. He took care to inform
himself upon the subjects which came up for

legislation, and for this reason he was always listened to with respectful attention. Moreover, his genial manners and warmth of heart made him a general favorite among all his fellow legislators, whether they belonged to his party or to the opposition.

Again, in the session of 1860–61, being also a member of the Senate, he took a prominent part in such measures as were proposed to uphold the National Government, menaced by the representative men of the South. He was among the foremost in declaring that the integrity of the Union must be protected at all hazards, and declared that it was the right and duty of the Government to coerce the seceded States.

When the President's call for seventy-five thousand men was made public, and announcement was made to the Ohio Senate, Senator Garfield sprang to his feet, and amid loud applause moved that "twenty thousand troops and three millions of money" should be at once voted as Ohio's quota! He closed his speech by offering his services to Governor Dennison in any capacity.

This offer the Governor bore in mind, and on the 14th of August, 1861, Garfield was offered the Lieutenant-Colonelcy of the Forty-second Ohio regiment, which he had been instrumental in forming.

It was a serious moment for Garfield. The acceptance of this commission would derange all his cherished plans. It would separate him from his wife and child, and from the loved institution of which he was the head. He must bid farewell to the calm, studious life, which he so much enjoyed, and spend days and months in the camp, liable at any moment to fall the victim of an enemy's bullet.

Suppose he should be killed? His wife would have no provision but the small sum of three thousand dollars, which he had been able by great economy to save from his modest salary.

He hesitated, but it was not for long. He was not a man to shrink from the call of duty. Before moving he wrote to a friend:

"I regard my life as given to the country. I am only anxious to make as much of it as possible before the mortgage on it is foreclosed."

CHAPTER XXI.
A DIFFICULT DUTY.

Having made up his mind to serve his country in the field, Garfield immediately wrote to the Governor accepting the appointment.

The regiment to which he was assigned was recruited from the same counties which he represented in the State Senate. A large number of the officers and privates had been connected as students with Hiram College, and were personally known to Garfield.

His first step was to qualify himself for his new position. Of the art and mystery of war the young scholar knew little, but he was no worse off than many another whom the exigencies of his country summoned from peaceful pursuits to the tented field and the toilsome march. It was probably the only office which he ever assumed without suitable qualifications. But it was not in his nature to undertake any duties without endeavoring to fit himself for their discharge.

His method of studying the art of war was curious and original. Falling back on his old trade of carpenter, he brought "his saw and jack-plane again into play, fashioned companies, officers and non-commissioned officers out of maple blocks, and with these wooden-headed troops he thoroughly mastered the infantry tactics in his quarters." There was this advantage in his method, that his toy troops were thoroughly manageable.

The next step was to organize a school for the officers of his regiment, requiring thorough recitation in the tactics, while their teacher illustrated the maneuvers by the blocks he had prepared for his own instruction. He was obliged to begin with the officers, that they might be qualified to assist him in instructing the men under their command. He was then able to institute regimental, squad, skirmish, and bayonet drill, and kept his men at these exercises from six to eight hours daily till the Forty-second won the reputation of being the best drilled regiment to be found in Ohio.

My boy readers will be reminded of the way in which he taught geometry in one of his winter schools, preparing himself at night for the lesson of the next day. I would like to call their attention also to the thoroughness with which he did everything. Though previously ignorant of military tactics he instructed his regiment in them thoroughly, believing that whatever was worth doing at all was worth doing well.

He was appointed Lieutenant-Colonel, but by the time his organization was completed he was promoted to the Colonelcy.

At last the preliminary work was completed. His men, an undisciplined body when he took them in hand, had become trained soldiers, but as yet they had not received what Napoleon III. called the "baptism of fire." It is all very well to march and countermarch, and practice the ordinary evolutions like militia-men at a muster, but how was the regiment, how was its scholarly commander likely to act in the field?

On the 14th of December orders for the field were received by Colonel Garfield's command, stationed at Camp Chase.

Then came the trial of parting with wife and mother and going forth to battle and danger. To his mother, whose highest ambition had been that her son should be a scholar, it was doubtless a keen disappointment that his settled prospects should be so broken up; but she, too, was patriotic, and she quietly said: "Go, my son, your life belongs to your country."

Colonel Garfield's orders were to report to General Buell at Louisville. He moved his regiment by way of Cincinnati to Catlettsburg, Kentucky, a town at the junction of the Big Sandy and the Ohio, and was enabled to report to his commander on the 19th of December.

Then, for the first time, he learned what was the nature of the duty that was assigned to him. It was no less than to save Kentucky to the Union.

A border State, with an interest in slavery, public opinion was divided, and it was uncertain to which side it would incline. The Confederates understood the value of the prize, and they had taken measures, which promised to be successful, to wrest it from the Union. The task had been committed to Gen. Humphrey Marshall, who had invaded Eastern Kentucky from the Virginia border, and had already advanced as far north as Prestonburg.

Gen. Marshall fortified a strong natural position near Paintville, and overran the whole Piedmont region. This region contained few slaves—but one in twenty-five of the whole population. It was inhabited by a brave rural population, more closely resembling their Northern than their Southern neighbors. Among these people Marshall sent stump orators to fire them with enthusiasm for the Confederate cause. Such men would make valuable soldiers and must be won over if possible.

So all that portion of the State was in a ferment. It looked as if it would be lost to the Union. Marshall was daily increasing the number of his forces, preparing either to intercept Buell, and prevent his advance into Tennessee, or, cutting off his communications, with the assistance of Beauregard, to crush him between them.

To Colonel Garfield, an inexperienced civilian, who had only studied military tactics by the aid of wooden blocks, and who had never been under fire, it was proposed to meet Marshall, a trained soldier, to check his advance, and drive him from the State. This would have been formidable enough if he had been provided with an equal number of soldiers; but this was far from being the case. He had but twenty-five hundred men to aid him in his difficult work, and of these eleven hundred, under Colonel Craven, were a hundred miles away, at Paris, Kentucky, and this hundred miles was no level plain, but a rough, mountainous country, infested with guerrillas and occupied by a disloyal people.

Of course, the first thing to be done was to connect with Colonel Craven, but, considering the distance and the nature of the country to be traversed, it was a most difficult problem. The chances were that Gen. Marshall, with his vastly superior force, would attack the two bodies of soldiers separately, and crush them before a union could be effected.

Gen. Buell explained how matters stood to the young colonel of volunteers, and ended thus:

"That is what you have to do, Colonel Garfield—drive Marshall from Kentucky, and you see how much depends on your action. Now go to your quarters, think of it overnight, and come here in the morning and tell me how you will do it."

In college Garfield had been called upon to solve many difficult problems in the higher mathematics, but it is doubtful whether he ever encountered a more knotty problem than this one.

He and Colonel Craven represented two little boys of feeble strength, unable to combine their efforts, who were called upon to oppose and capture a big boy of twice their size, who knew a good deal more about fighting than they did.

No wonder the young colonel felt perplexed. But he did not give up. It was not his way. He resolved to consider whether anything could be done, and what.

My chief object in writing this volume being to commend its subject as an example for boys, I think it right to call attention to this trait which he possessed in a conspicuous degree. Brought face to face with difficulty—with what might almost be called the impossible, he did not say, "Oh, I can't do it. It is impossible." He went home to devise a plan.

First of all, it was important that he should know something of the intervening country—its conformation, its rivers and streams, if there were any. So, on his way to his room he sought a book-store and bought a rude map of Kentucky, and then, shutting himself up in his room, while others were asleep, he devoted himself to a lesson in geography. With more care than he had ever used in school, he familiarized himself with the geography of the country in which he was to operate, and then set himself to devise some feasible plan of campaign.

It was a hard problem, and required still more anxious thought, because the general to whom he was to report it, was, unlike himself, a man thoroughly trained in the art of war.

The next morning, according to orders, he sought again his commanding officer.

Gen. Buell was a man of great reticence and severe military habits, and if the plan were weak or foolish, as might well be from the utter lack of experience of the young officer who was to make it, he would unhesitatingly say so.

As Garfield laid his rude map and roughly outlined plan on the table, and explained his conception of the campaign, he watched anxiously to see how Gen. Buell was impressed by it. But the general was a man who knew how to veil his thoughts. He waited in silence till Garfield had finished, only asking a brief question now and then, and at the end, without expressing his opinion one way or the other, merely said: "Colonel Garfield, your orders will be sent you at six o'clock this evening."

Garfield was not compelled to wait beyond that hour.

Promptly the order came, organizing the Eighteenth Brigade of the Army of the Ohio, under the command of Colonel Garfield, with a letter of instructions, embodying essentially the plan submitted by the young officer in the morning.

When Garfield set out with his command the next morning, Gen. Buell said to him at parting:

"Colonel, you will be at so great a distance from me, and communication will be so difficult, that I must commit all matters of detail and much of the fate of the campaign to your discretion. I shall hope to hear a good account of you."

CHAPTER XXII.
JOHN JORDAN'S DANGEROUS JOURNEY.

Col. Garfield had already sent on his regiment in advance to Louisa, twenty-eight miles up the Big Sandy.

There he joined them on the 24th, having waited at Catlettsburg only long enough to forward to them necessary supplies.

The arrival of the regiment was opportune, for the district was thoroughly alarmed. A regiment had been stationed there—the Fourteenth Kentucky—but had hastily retreated to the mouth of the river during the night of the 19th, under the impression that Marshall was advancing with his forces to drive them into the Ohio. It was a false alarm, but the Union citizens were very much alarmed, and were preparing with their families to cross the river for safety. With the appearance of Garfield's regiment a feeling of security returned.

I am anxious to make plain to my boy readers the manner in which the young colonel managed his campaign. I think they will have no difficulty in understanding that Garfield had two very difficult things to accomplish. Colonel Craven knew nothing of Garfield's advance, nor of his plans. It was necessary to inform him. Again, if possible, a junction must be effected. The first was difficult, because the intervening country was infested with roving bands of guerrillas, and a messenger must take his life in his hands. How, again, could a junction be effected in the face of a superior enemy, liable to fall upon either column and crush it?

Obviously the first thing was to find a messenger.

Garfield applied to Col. Moore of the Fourteenth Kentucky, and made known his need.

"Have you a man," he asked, "who will die rather than fail or betray us?"

"Yes," answered the Kentuckian, after a pause, "I think I have. His name is John Jordan, and he comes from the head of the Blaine."

This was a small stream which entered the Big Sandy, a short distance from the town.

At the request of Garfield, Jordan was sent for. In a short time he entered the tent of the Union commander.

This John Jordan was a remarkable man, and well known in all that region. He was of Scotch descent, and possessed some of the best traits of his Scotch ancestry. He was a born actor, a man of undoubted courage, fertile in expedients, and devoted to the Union cause.

Garfield was a judge of men, and he was impressed in the man's favor at first sight. He describes Jordan as a tall, gaunt, sallow man, about thirty years of age, with gray eyes, a fine falsetto voice, and a face of wonderful expressiveness. To the young colonel he was a new type of man, but withal a man whom he was convinced that he could trust.

"Why did you come into this war?" he asked, with some curiosity.

"To do my share, colonel, and I've made a bargain with the Lord. I gave Him my life to start with, and if He has a mind to take it, it's His. I've nothing to say agin it."

"You mean you have come into the war, not expecting to get out of it alive?"

"Yes, colonel."

"You know what I want you to do. Will you die rather than let this dispatch be taken?"

"I will."

Garfield looked into the man's face, and he read unmistakable sincerity.

He felt that the man could be trusted, and he said so.

The dispatch was written upon tissue paper. It was then rolled into the form of a bullet, coated with warm lead, and given into the hands of the messenger. He was provided with a carbine and a brace of revolvers, and when the moon was down, he mounted his horse in the darkness and set out on his perilous journey.

It would not do to ride in the daytime, for inevitably he would be stopped, or shot down. By day he must hide in the woods, and travel only at night.

His danger was increased by the treachery of one of his own comrades of the Fourteenth Kentucky, and he was followed by a band of guerrillas in the Confederate interest. Of this, however, Jordan was not apprised, and supposing himself secure he sought shelter and concealment at the house of a man whom he knew to be loyal. Near enough to see, but not to be seen, the guerrillas waited till the tired messenger was sleeping, and then coming boldly out of the woods, surrounded the house.

In a fright the good housewife ran up to his chamber, and shook the sleeping man.

"Wake for your life!" she said. "The guerrillas are outside, clamoring for you. I have locked the doors, but I can not keep them out long."

Jordan had thrown himself on the bed with his clothes on. He knew that he was liable to be surprised, and in such an event time was most valuable. Though awakened from a sound sleep, he had all his wits about him.

"Thank you," said he. "I have a favor to ask in the name of our cause."

"Be quick, then," said the woman. "They are bursting open the door."

"Take this bullet. It contains a secret dispatch, which, if I am killed, I enjoin upon you to convey to Colonel Craven, at Paris. Will you do it?"

"If I can."

"Then I am off."

The door burst open, but he made a sudden dash, and escaped capture. He headed for the woods, amid a volley of bullets, but none of them reached him. Once he turned round, and fired an answering shot. He did not stop to see if it took effect, but it was the messenger of Death. One of the guerrillas reeled, and measured his length upon the ground, dead in a moment.

Fleet as a deer the brave scout pushed on till he got within the protecting shadows of the friendly woods. There they lost the trail, and though he saw them from his place of conceal-ment, he was himself unseen.

"Curse him!" said the disappointed leader.

"He must have sunk into the earth, or vanished into the air."

"If he's sunk into the earth, that is where we want him," answered another, with grim humor.

"You will find I am not dead yet!" said the hidden scout to himself. "I shall live to trouble you yet."

He passed the remainder of the day in the woods, fearing that his pursuers might still be lingering about.

"If there were only two or three, I'd come out and face 'em," he said, "but the odds are too great. I must skulk back in the darkness, and get back the bullet."

Night came on, and the woman who had saved him, heard a low tapping at the door. It might be an enemy, and she advanced, and opened it with caution. A figure, seen indistinctly in the darkness, stood before her.

"Who are you?" she asked doubtfully.

"Don't be afraid, ma'am, it's only me."

"And you—"

"Are the man you saved this morning!"

"God be thanked! Then you were not killed?"

"Do I look like a dead man? No, my time hasn't come yet. I foiled 'em in the wood, and there I have spent all day. Have you any victuals, for I am famished?"

"Yes, come in."

"I can not stay. I will take what you have and leave at once, for the villains may be lurkin' round here somewhere. But first, the bullet! have you that safe?"

"Here it is."

The scout put it in his pocket, and taking in his hand a paper box of bread and meat which his loyal hostess brought him, resumed his hazardous journey.

He knew that there were other perils to encounter, unless he was particularly fortunate, but he had a heart prepared for any fate. The perils came, but he escaped them with adroitness, and at midnight of the following day he was admitted into the presence of Colonel Craven.

Surely this was no common man, and his feat was no common one.

In forty-eight hours, traveling only by night, he had traversed one hundred miles with a rope round his neck, and without the prospect of special reward. For he was but a private, and received but a private's pay—thirteen dollars a month, a shoddy uniform, and hard-tack, when he could get it.

Colonel Craven opened the bullet, and read the dispatch.

It was dated "Louisa, Kentucky, December 24, midnight"; and directed him to move at once with his regiment (the Fortieth Ohio, eight hundred strong) by way of Mount Sterling and McCormick's Gap, to Prestonburg. He was to encumber his men with as few rations as possible, since the safety of his command depended on his celerity. He was also requested to notify Lieutenant-Colonel Woodford, at Stamford, and direct him to join the march with his three hundred cavalry.

On the following morning Col. Craven's column began to move. The scout waited till night, and then set out on his return. The reader will be glad to learn that the brave man rejoined his regiment.

CHAPTER XXIII.
GARFIELD'S BOLD STRATEGY.

Garfield didn't wait for the scout's return. He felt that no time was to be lost. The expedition which he had planned was fraught with peril, but it was no time for timid counsels.

On the morning following Jordan's departure he set out up the river, halting at George's Creek, only twenty miles from Marshall's intrenched position. As the roads along the Big Sandy were impassable for trains, and unsafe on account of the nearness of the enemy, he decided to depend mainly upon water navigation for the transportation of his supplies.

The Big Sandy finds its way to the Ohio through the roughest and wildest spurs of the Cumberland Mountains, and is a narrow, fickle stream. At low-water it is not navigable above Louisa, except for small flat-boats pushed by hand. At high-water small steamers can reach Piketon, one hundred and twenty miles from the mouth; but when there are heavy freshets the swift current, filled with floating timber, and the overhanging trees which almost touch one another from the opposite banks, render navigation almost impracticable. This was enough to intimidate a man less in earnest than Garfield. He did not hesitate, but gathering together ten days' rations, he chartered two small steamers, and seizing all the flat-boats he could lay hands on, took his army wagons apart, and loaded them, with his forage and provisions, upon the flat-boats.

Just as he was ready to start he received an unexpected reinforcement. Captain Bent, of the Fourteenth Kentucky, entering Garfield's tent, said to him, "Colonel, there's a man outside who says he knows you. Bradley Brown, a rebel thief and scoundrel."

"Bradley Brown," repeated Garfield, puzzled. "I don't remember any such name."

"He has lived near the head of the Blaine, and been a boatman on the river. He says he knew you on the canal in Ohio."

"Oh, yes, I remember him now; bring him in."

Brown was ushered into the general's tent. He was clad in homespun, and spattered from head to foot with mud, but he saw in Garfield only the friend of earlier days, and hurrying up to him, gave him a hearty grasp of the hand, exclaiming, "Jim, old feller, how are yer?"

Garfield received him cordially, but added, "What is this I hear, Brown? Are you a rebel?"

"Yes," answered the new-comer, "I belong to Marshall's force, and I've come straight from his camp to spy out your army."

"Well, you go about it queerly," said Garfield, puzzled.

"Wait till you are alone, colonel. Then I'll tell you about it."

Col. Bent said in an undertone to Garfield, as he left the tent, "Don't trust him, colonel; I know him as a thief and a rebel."

This was the substance of Brown's communication. As soon as he heard that James A. Garfield was in command of the Union forces, it instantly struck him that it must be his old comrade of the canal, for whom he still cherished a strong attachment. He was in the rebel camp, but in reality cared little which side was successful, and determined out of old friendship to help Garfield if he could.

Concealing his design, he sought Marshall, and proposed to visit the Union camp as a spy, mentioning his former intimacy with Garfield. Gen. Marshall readily acceded to his plan, not suspecting that it was his real purpose to tell Garfield all he knew about the rebel force. He proceeded to give the colonel valuable information on this subject.

When he had finished, Garfield said, "I advise you to go back to Marshall."

"Go back to him, colonel? Why, he would hang me to the first tree."

"Not if you tell him all about my strength and intended movements."

"But how kin I? I don't know a thing. I was brought into the camp blindfolded."

"Still you can guess. Suppose you tell him that I shall march to-morrow straight for his camp, and in ten days be upon him."

"You'd be a fool, colonel, to do that, and he 'trenched so strongly, unless you had twenty thousand men."

"I haven't got that number. Guess again."

"Well, ten thousand."

"That will do for a guess. Now to-day I shall keep you locked up, and to-morrow you can go back to Marshall."

At nightfall Brown went back to the rebel camp, and his report was made in accordance with Garfield's suggestions.

The fact was, that deducting those sick and on garrison duty, Garfield's little army amounted to but fourteen hundred in place of the ten thousand reported to the rebel commander. This little army was set in motion the next day. It was a toilsome and discouraging march, over roads knee-deep in mire, and the troops necessarily made but slow progress, being frequently obliged to halt. Some days they succeeded in making but five or six miles. On the 6th of January, however, they arrived within seven miles of Paintville. Here while Garfield was trying to catch a few hours' sleep, in a wretched log hut, he was roused by Jordan, the scout, who had just managed to reach the camp.

"Have you seen Craven?" asked Garfield eagerly.

"Yes; he can't be more'n two days behind me, nohow."

"God bless you, Jordan! You have done us great service," said Garfield, warmly, feeling deeply relieved by this important news.

"Thank ye, colonel. That's more pay 'n I expected."

In the morning another horseman rode up to the Union camp. He was a messenger direct from Gen. Buell. He brought with him an intercepted letter from Marshall to his wife, revealing the important fact that the Confederate general had five thousand men—forty-four hundred infantry and six hundred cavalry—with twelve pieces of artillery, and that he was daily expecting an attack from a Union force of ten thousand.

It was clear that Brown had been true, and that it was from him Gen. Marshall had received this trustworthy intelligence of the strength of the Union army.

Garfield decided not to communicate the contents of this letter, lest his officers should be alarmed at the prospect of attacking a force so much superior. He called a council, however, and put this question:

"Shall we march at once, or wait the coming of Craven?"

All but one were in favor of waiting, but Garfield adopted the judgment of this one.

"Forward it is!" he said. "Give the order."

I will only state the plan of Garfield's attack in a general way. There were three roads that led to Marshall's position—one to the east, one to the west, and one between the two. These three roads were held by strong Confederate pickets.

Now, it was Garfield's policy to keep Marshall deceived as to his strength. For this reason, he sent a small body to drive in the enemy's pickets, as if to attack Paintville. Two hours after, a similar force, with the same orders, were sent on the road to the westward, and two hours later still, a small force was sent on the middle road. The first pickets, retreating in confusion, fled to the camp, with the intelligence that a large body of Union troops were on their way to make an attack. Similar tidings were brought by the two other bodies of pickets, and Marshall, in dismay, was led to believe that he was menaced by superior numbers, and hastily abandoned Paintville, and Garfield, moving his men rapidly over the central route, occupied the town.

Gen. Marshall would have been intensely mortified had he known that this large Union army was little more than one-fourth the size of his own.

But his alarm was soon increased. On the evening of the 8th of January, a spy entered his camp, and reported that Craven, with *thirty-three hundred men*, was within twelve hours' march at the westward.

The big general (he weighed three hundred pounds) was panic-stricken. Believing Garfield's force to number ten thousand, this reinforcement would carry his strength up to over thirteen thousand. Ruin and defeat, as he fancied, stared him in the face, for how could his five thousand men encounter nearly three times their number? They would, of course, be overwhelmed. There was safety only in flight.

So the demoralized commander gave orders to break camp, and retreated precipitately, abandoning or burning a large portion of his supplies.

Garfield saw the fires, and guessed what had happened, being in the secret of Marshall's delusion. He mounted his horse, and, with a thousand men, entered the deserted camp at nine in the evening. The stores that were yet unconsumed he rescued from destruction for the use of his own army.

In order to keep up the delusion, he sent off a detachment to harass the retreat of his ponderous adversary and fill his mind with continued disquiet.

The whole thing was a huge practical joke, but not one that the rebels were likely to enjoy. Fancy a big boy of eighteen fleeing in dismay from a small urchin of eight, and we have a parallel to this flight of Gen. Marshall from an intrenched position, with five thousand troops, when his opponent could muster but fourteen hundred men in the open field.

Thus far, I think, it will be agreed that Colonel Garfield was a strategist of the first order. His plan required a boldness and dash which, under the circumstances, did him the greatest credit.

The next morning Colonel Craven arrived, and found, to his amazement, that Garfield, single-handed, had forced his formidable enemy from his strong position, and was in triumphant possession of the deserted rebel camp.

CHAPTER XXIV.
THE BATTLE OF MIDDLE CREEK.

Col. Garfield has gained a great advantage, but he knows that it must be followed up. His ambition is not satisfied. He means to force a fight with Marshall, despite the odds.

He has been reinforced, but Craven's men are completely exhausted by their long and toilsome march. They are hardly able to drag one foot after the other. Garfield knows this, but he explains to his men what he proposes to do. He orders those who have strength to come forward. Of the men under his immediate command seven hundred obey the summons. Of Craven's weary followers four hundred heroic men volunteer to accompany him.

So at noon of the 9th, with eleven hundred men, Garfield sets out for Prestonburg, sending all his available cavalry to follow the line of the enemy's retreat. At nine o'clock that night, after a march of eighteen miles, he reaches the mouth of Abbott's Creek with his eleven hundred men. He hears that his opponent is encamped three miles higher up on the same stream. He sends an order back to Lieutenant-Colonel Sheldon, who is left in command at Paintville, to bring up every available man with all possible dispatch, for he intends to force a battle in the morning.

He requires to know the disposition of Marshall's forces, and here the gallant scout, John Jordan, again is of service to him. While a dozen Confederates were grinding at a mill, they were surprised by as many Union men, who, taking them by surprise, captured their corn, and made them prisoners. Jordan eyed the miller with a critical eye, and a plan was instantly formed. The miller was a tall, gaunt man, and his clothes would fit the scout. He takes a fancy to exchange raiment with the miller. Then, smearing his face with meal, he goes back to the Confederate camp in a new character. Even if he is surprised he will escape suspicion, for the miller is a pronounced disunionist, and he looks his very image.

His midnight ramble enabled him to learn precisely what it was important for Garfield to know. He found out their exact position, and that they had laid an ambuscade for the Union commander. They were waiting for him, strongly posted on a semicircular hill at the forks of Middle Creek, on both sides of the road, with cannon commanding its whole length, hidden by the trees and underbrush.

"They think they've got you, general," said Jordan. "They're waitin' for you as a cat waits for a mouse."

Upon a steep ridge called Abbott's Hill, the Union soldiers, tired and sleepy, had thrown themselves upon the wet ground. There was a dense fog, shutting out the moon and stars, and shrouding the lonely mountain in darkness. The rain was driven in blinding gusts into the faces of the shivering men, and tired as they were they hailed with joy the coming of morning. For more than one brave man it was destined to be his last day upon earth.

At four o'clock they started on their march. About daybreak, while rounding a hill, their advance guard was charged upon by a body of Confederate horsemen. In return Garfield gave the Confederates a volley, that sent them reeling up the valley.

It was clear that the main body of the enemy was not far away. To determine this Garfield sent forward a body of skirmishers to draw the fire of the enemy. He succeeded, for a twelve-pound shell whistled above the trees, then plowed up the hill, and buried itself in the ground at the feet of the little band of skirmishers.

Noon came, and Garfield made the necessary preparations for battle. He could not have been without apprehension, for he knew, though the enemy did not, that their force was far superior to his. He sent forward his mounted escort of twelve men to make a charge and draw the enemy's fire. His plan succeeded. Another shell whistled over their heads, and the long roll of five thousand muskets was heard.

It was certainly a remarkable battle, when we consider that a small band of eleven hundred men without cannon had undertaken to attack a force of five thousand, supported by twelve pieces of artillery, charging up a rocky hill, over stumps, over stones, over fallen trees, and over high intrenchments.

The battle was fought on the margin of Middle Creek, a narrow, rapid stream, and three miles from where it finds its way into the Big Sandy, through the sharp spurs of the Cumberland Mountain. A rocky road, not ten feet in width, winds along this stream, and on its two banks abrupt ridges, with steep and rocky sides, overgrown with trees and underbrush, shut closely down upon the road and the little streamlet. At twelve o'clock Garfield had gained the crest of the ridge at the right of the road, and the charge of his handful of horsemen had drawn Marshall's fire, and disclosed his actual position.

The main force of the Confederates occupied the crests of the two ridges at the left of the stream, but a strong detachment was posted on the right, and a battery of twelve pieces held the forks of the creek, and commanded the approach of the Union army. It was Marshall's plan to drive Garfield along the road, and then, taking him between two enfilading fires, to surround and utterly destroy him. But his hasty fire betrayed his design, and unmasked his entire position.

Garfield acted with promptness and decision. A hundred undergraduates, recruited from his own college, were ordered to cross the stream, climb the ridge whence the fire had been hottest, and bring on the battle. Boldly the little band plunged into the creek, the icy water up to their waists, and clinging to the trees and underbrush, climbed the rocky ascent. Half-way up the ridge the fire of at least two thousand rifles opens upon them; but, springing from tree to tree, they press on, and at last reach the summit. Then suddenly the hill is gray with Confederates, who, rising from ambush, pour their deadly volleys into the little band of only one hundred. In a moment they waver, but their leader calls out, "Every man to a tree! Give them as good as they send, my boys!"

The Confederates, behind rocks and a rude intrenchment, are obliged to expose their heads to take aim at the advancing column; but the Union troops, posted behind the huge oaks and maples, can stand erect, and load and fire, fully protected. Though they are outnumbered ten to one, the contest is therefore, for a time, not so very unequal.

But soon the Confederates, exhausted with the obstinate resistance, rush from cover, and charge upon the little handful with the bayonet. Slowly they are driven down the hill, and two of them fall to the ground wounded. One never rises; the other, a lad of only eighteen, is shot through the thigh, and one of his comrades turns back to bear him to a place of safety. The advancing Confederates are within thirty feet, when one of them fires, and his bullet strikes a tree directly above the head of the Union soldier. He turns, levels his musket, and the Confederate is in eternity. Then the rest are upon him; but, zigzagging from tree to tree, he is soon with his driven column. But not far are the brave boys driven. A few rods lower down they hear the voice of the brave Captain Williams, their leader.

"To the trees again, my boys!" he cries. "We may as well die here as in Ohio!"

To the trees they go, and in a moment the advancing horde is checked, and then rolled backward. Up the hill they turn, firing as they go, and the little band follows. Soon the Confederates reach the spot where the Hiram boy lies wounded, and one of them says: "Boy, give me your musket."

"Not the gun, but its contents," cries the boy, and the Confederate falls mortally wounded. Another raises his weapon to brain the prostrate lad, but he too falls, killed with his comrade's own rifle. And all this is done while the hero-boy is on the ground, bleeding. An hour afterward his comrades bear the boy to a sheltered spot on the other side of the streamlet, and then the first word of complaint escapes him. As they are taking off his leg, he says, in his agony, "Oh, what will mother do?"

Poor boy! At that terrible moment, in the throes of his fierce agony, he thought not of himself, but of the mother at home, who was dependent on his exertions for a livelihood. For in war it is not alone the men in the field who are called upon to suffer, but the mothers, the wives, and the children, left at home, whose hearts are rent with anxiety—to whom, at any moment, may come the tidings of the death of their loved one.

On a rocky height, commanding the field, Garfield watched the tide of battle. He saw that it was unequal, and that there was danger that his troops would be overmatched. He saw that they were being driven, and that they would lose the hill if not supported.

Instantly he ordered to the rescue five hundred of the Ohio Fortieth and Forty-second, under Major Pardee and Colonel Craven. They dashed boldly into the stream, holding their cartridge-boxes above their heads, and plunged into the fight, shouting:

"Hurrah for Williams and the Hiram boys!"

But their position was most critical, for shot, and shell, and canister, and the fire of four thousand muskets are now concentrated upon them.

"This will never do!" cries Garfield. "Who will volunteer to carry the other mountain?"

Colonel Munroe, of the Twenty-second Kentucky, responded quickly, "We will. We know every inch of the ground."

"Go in, then," cries Garfield, "and give them Columbia!"

I have not space to record the varying fortunes of the day. For five hours the contest rages. By turns the Union forces are driven back, and then, with a brave charge, they regain their lost ground, and from behind rocks and trees pour in their murderous volleys. The battle began at noon, and when the sun sets on the brief winter day it is still unfinished.

Posted on a projecting rock, in full sight of both armies, stands the Union commander—his head uncovered, his hair streaming in the wind, and his heart full of alternate hopes and fears. It looks as if the day were lost—as if the gallant eleven hundred were conquered at last, when, at a critical moment, the starry banner is seen waving over an advancing host. It is Sheldon and reinforcements—long and anxiously expected! Their shouts are taken up by the eleven hundred! The enemy see them and are panic-stricken.

The day is won!

CHAPTER XXV.
THE PERILOUS TRIP UP THE BIG SANDY.

I have followed Col. Garfield through the Kentucky campaign, not because it compared in importance with many other military operations of the war, but because in its conduct he displayed in a remarkable degree some of the traits by which he was distinguished. From a military point of view it may be criticised. His attack upon an enemy far his superior in numbers, and in a more favorable position, would scarcely have been undertaken by an officer of more military experience. Yet, once undertaken, it was carried through with remarkable dash and brilliancy, and the strategy displayed was of a high order.

I must find room for the address issued to his little army on the day succeeding the battle, for it tells, in brief, the story of the campaign:

SOLDIERS OF THE EIGHTEENTH BRIGADE: I am proud of you all! In four weeks you have marched, some eighty and some a hundred miles, over almost impassable roads. One night in four you have slept, often in the storm, with only a wintry sky above your heads. You have marched in the face of a foe of more than double your number—led on by chiefs who have won a national reputation under the old flag—intrenched in hills of his own choosing, and strengthened by all the appliances of military art. With no experience but the consciousness of your own manhood, you have driven him from his strongholds, pursued his inglorious flight, and compelled him to meet you in battle. When forced to fight, he sought the shelter of rocks and hills. You drove him from his position, leaving scores of his bloody dead unburied. His artillery thundered against you, but you compelled him to flee by the light of his burning stores, and to leave even the banner of his rebellion behind him. I greet you as brave men. Our common country will not forget you. She will not forget the sacred dead who fell beside you, nor those of your comrades who won scars of honor on the field.

I have recalled you from the pursuit that you may regain vigor for still greater exertions. Let no one tarnish his well-earned honor by any act unworthy an American soldier. Remember your duties as American citizens, and sacredly respect the rights and property of those with whom you have come in contact. Let it not be said that good men dread the approach of an American army.

Officers and soldiers, your duty has been nobly done. For this I thank you.

The battle had been won, but the victorious army was in jeopardy. They had less than three days' rations, and there were great difficulties in the way of procuring a further supply. The rainy season had made the roads impassable for all but horsemen.

Still there was the river. But the Big Sandy was now swollen beyond its banks, and the rapid current was filled with floating logs and uptorn trees. The oldest and most experienced boatmen shook their heads, and would not attempt the perilous voyage.

What was to be done?

Col. Garfield had with him Brown, the scout and ex-canal-boatman, who had returned from reconnoitering Marshall's camp, with a bullet through his hat. Garfield asked his advice.

"It's which and t'other, General Jim," he answered, "starvin' or drownin'. I'd rather drown nur starve. So gin the word, and, dead or alive, I'll git down the river!"

Garfield gave the word, but he did not let the brave scout go alone. Together in a small skiff they "got down the river." It was no light task. The Big Sandy was now a raging torrent, sixty feet in depth, and, in many places, above the tops of the tall trees which grew along its margin. In some deep and narrow gorges, where the steep banks shut down upon the stream, these trees had been undermined at the roots, and, falling inward, had locked their arms together, forming a net-work that well-nigh prevented the passage of the small skiff and its two navigators. Where a small skiff could scarcely pass, could they run a large steamboat loaded with provisions?

Other men might ask that question, but not the backwoods boy who had learned navigation on the waters of the Ohio and Pennsylvania Canal. He pushed to the mouth of the river, and there took possession of the *Sandy Valley*, a small steamer in the quartermaster's service. Loading her with supplies, he set about starting up the river, but the captain of the boat declared the thing was impossible. Not stopping to argue the point, Garfield ordered him and his crew on board, and *himself taking the helm*, set out up the river.

Brown he stationed at the bow, where, with a long fending-pole in his hand, he was to keep one eye on the floating logs and uprooted trees, the other on the chicken-hearted captain.

The river surged and boiled and whirled against the boat, tossing her about as if she were a cockle-shell. With every turn of her wheel she trembled from stem to stern, and with a full head of steam could only stagger along at the rate of three miles an hour. When night came the captain begged to tie up till morning, for breasting that flood in the dark was sheer madness; but Brown cried out, "Put her ahead, Gineral Jim," and Garfield clutched the helm and drove her on through the darkness.

Soon they came to a sudden bend in the stream, where the swift current formed a furious whirlpool, and this catching the laboring boat, whirled her suddenly round, and drove her, head on, into the quicksands. Mattocks were plied, and excavations made round the imbedded bow, and the bowman uttered oaths

loud enough to have raised a small earth-
quake; but still the boat was immovable. She
was stuck fast in the mud, and every effort
to move her was fruitless. Garfield ordered a
small boat to be lowered, and take a line to
the other bank, by which to warp the steamer
free; but the captain and now the crew pro-
tested it was certain death to attempt to cross
that foaming torrent at midnight.

They might as well have repeated to him
the Creed and the Ten Commandments, for
Garfield himself sprang into the boat and
called to Brown to follow. He took the helm
and laid her bow across the stream, but the
swift current swept them downward. After
incredible labor they made the opposite bank,
but far below the steamboat. Closely hugging
the shore, they now crept up the stream, and
fastening the line to a tree, rigged a windlass,
and finally warped the vessel again into deep
water.

All that night, and all the next day, and all
the following night they struggled with the
furious river, Garfield never but once leaving
the helm, and then for only a few hours' sleep,
which he snatched in his clothes in the daytime. At last they rounded to at the Union
camp, and then went up a cheer that might
have been heard all over Kentucky. His waiting men, frantic with joy, seized their glorious
commander, and were with difficulty prevented from bearing him on their shoulders to his
quarters.

The little army was saved from starvation by the canal-boy, who had not forgotten his old trade. He had risked his life a dozen times over in making the perilous trip, which has been so graphically described in the passages I have quoted. But for his early and humble experience, he never would have been able to bring the little steamer up the foaming river. Little did he dream in the days when, as a boy, he guided the *Evening Star*, that fifteen years hence, an officer holding an important command he would use the knowledge then acquired to save a famishing army. We can not wonder that his men should have been devotedly attached to such a commander.

I have said that the Kentucky campaign was not one of the most important operations of the civil war, but its successful issue was most welcome, coming at the time it did. It came after a series of disasters, which had produced widespread despondency, and even dimmed the courage of President Lincoln. It kindled hope in the despondent, and nerved patriotic arms to new and vigorous efforts.

"Why did Garfield, in two weeks, do what it would have taken one of you Regular folks two months to accomplish?" asked the President, of a distinguished army officer.

"Because he was not educated at West Point," answered the officer, laughing.

"No," replied Mr. Lincoln; "that wasn't the reason. It was because, when a boy, he had to work for a living."

This was literally true. To his struggling boyhood and early manhood, and the valuable experience it brought him, Garfield was indebted for the strength and practical knowledge which brought him safely through a campaign conducted against fearful odds.

His country was not ungrateful. He received the thanks of the commanding general for services which "called into action the highest qualities of a soldier—fortitude, perseverance, courage," and a few weeks later a commission as brigadier-general of volunteers, to date from the battle of Middle Creek.

So Jim Garfield, the canal-boy, has become a general. It is an important step upward, but where are others to come?

If this were designed to be a complete biography of General Garfield, I should feel it my duty to chronicle the important part he took in the battle of Chickamauga, where he acted as chief of staff to General Rosecranz, aiding his superior officer at a most critical point in the battle by advice which had an important influence in saving the day. I should like to describe the wonderful and perilous ride of three miles which he took, exposing his life at every moment, to warn General Thomas that he is out-flanked, and that at least seventy thousand men are closing down upon his right wing, to crush his twenty-five thousand to fragments. Sometimes I hope a poet, of fitting inspiration, will sing of that ride, and how, escaping from shot and shell, he plunged down the hill through the fiery storm, reaching Thomas in safety, though his noble horse at that moment fell dead at his feet. I can not spare time for the record, but must refer my young reader to the pages of Edmund Kirke, or General James S. Brisbin.

Other duties, and another important field of action, await Garfield, and we must hurry on. But, before doing so, I must not fail to record that the War Department, recognizing his important services at the battle of Chickamauga, sent him a fortnight later the commission of a major-general.

CHAPTER XXVI.
THE CANAL-BOY
BECOMES A CONGRESSMAN.

While Garfield was serving his country to the utmost of his ability in the field, the voters of the Nineteenth District of Ohio, in which he had his home, were called upon to select a man to represent them in Congress. It perhaps exceeds any other portion of the State in its devotion to the cause of education and the general intelligence of its inhabitants. The people were mostly of New England origin, and in selecting a representative they wanted a man who was fitted by education, as well as fidelity, to do them credit.

Their choice fell upon Garfield, who was known to them at home as the head of one of their chief institutions of learning, and whose reputation had not suffered in the field. They did not even consult him, but put him in nomination, and elected him by an overwhelming majority.

It was a gratifying compliment, for in our country an election to Congress is regarded as a high honor, which no one need be reluctant to accept. We have on record one of our most distinguished statesmen—John Quincy Adams—who, after filling the Presidential chair, was content to go back to Washington as a member of the House of Representatives from his district in Massachusetts. It was undoubtedly more in harmony with the desires and tastes of the young man—for he was still a young man—than service in the field. But he felt that that was not the question. Where was he more needed? The war was not over. Indeed, it seemed doubtful when it would be finished; and Garfield was now in a position to serve his country well as a military commander.

When on the march to Chattanooga, Garfield consulted Gen. Rosecranz, owning that he was perplexed in attempting to decide.

Rosecranz said: "The war is not yet over, nor will it be for some time to come. Many questions will arise in Congress which will require not only statesman-like treatment, but the advice of men having an acquaintance with military affairs. For that reason you will, I think, do as good service to the country in Congress as in the field. I not only think that you can accept the position with honor, but that it is your duty to do it."

He added, and we may be sure that his advice accorded with the personal judgment of the man whom he was addressing, "Be true to yourself, and you will make your mark before your country."

Some months were to elapse before he would require to go to Washington, for Congress was not to meet till December.

He went to Washington, undecided even yet whether to remain as a legislator, or to return to his old comrades in the army. He only wished to know where he could be of most service to his country, and he finally decided to lay the matter before President Lincoln.

Lincoln gave substantially the same advice as Rosecranz: "We need men who will help us carry the necessary war measures; and, besides, we are greatly lacking in men of military experience in the House to promote legislation about the army. It is your duty, therefore, to enter Congress."

When, on the 5th of December, 1863, Garfield took his seat in the House of Representatives, he was the youngest member of that body. The Military Committee was the most important committee of Congress, and he was put upon that, on account of his practical experience in the field. This, of course, brought him, though a new and young member, into immediate prominence, and his familiarity with the wants of the army enabled him to be of great service.

I do not propose to detail at tiresome length the legislative achievements of Gen. Garfield in the new position which he was destined to fill for eighteen years. I shall only refer to such as illustrate his characteristic devotion to duty without special regard to his own interests. He never hesitated to array himself in opposition to the popular will, if he thought the people were wrong. It was not long before an occasion came up which enabled him to assert his independence.

The country needed soldiers, and had inaugurated a system of bounties which should tempt men to join the ranks of the country's defenders. It was only a partial success. Some men, good and true, were led to join by the offer of a sum which made them more at ease about the comfort of their families, but many joined the service from mercenary considerations only, who seized the first opportunity to desert, and turning up in another locality, enlisted again and obtained a second bounty. These men obtained the name of bounty-jumpers, and there was a host of them. Yet the measure was popular with soldiers, and Congress was unanimously in favor of it. Great was the amazement of his fellow-members when the young member from the Nineteenth Ohio district rose in his seat and earnestly opposed it. He objected that the policy was ruinous, involving immense expense, while effecting little good. He claimed that the country had a right to the service of every one of its children at such a crisis, without hire and without reward.

But one man stood with him, so unpopular was the stand he had taken; but it was not long before the bounty system broke down, and Garfield's views were adopted.

Later on he had another chance to show his independence. President Lincoln, foreseeing that at a certain date not far ahead the time of enlistment of nearly half the army would expire, came before Congress and asked for power to draft men into service. It met with great opposition. "What! force men into the field! Why, we might as well live under a despotism!" exclaimed many; and the members of Congress, who knew how unpopular the measure would be among their constituents, defeated it by a two-thirds vote.

It was a critical juncture. As Lincoln had said in substance, all military operations would be checked. Not only could not the war be pushed, but the Government could not stand where it did. Sherman would have to come back from Atlanta, Grant from the Peninsula.

The voting was over, and the Government was despondent. Then it was that Garfield rose, and moving a reconsideration, made a speech full of fire and earnestness, and the House, carried by storm, passed the bill, and President Lincoln made a draft for half a million men.

Garfield knew that this action would be unpopular in his district. It might defeat his re-election; but that mattered not. The President had been assailed by the same argument, and had answered, "Gentlemen, it is not necessary that I should be reëlected, but it is necessary that I should put down this rebellion." With this declaration the young Congressman heartily sympathized.

Remonstrances did come from his district. Several of his prominent supporters addressed him a letter, demanding his resignation. He wrote them that he had acted according to his views of the needs of the country; that he was sorry his judgment did not agree with theirs, but that he must follow his own. He expected to live long enough to have them all confess that he was right.

It was about this time that he made his celebrated reply to Mr. Alexander Long, of Ohio, a
fellow Congressman, who proposed to yield everything and to recognize the Southern Confederacy.

The excitement was intense. In the midst of it
Garfield rose and made the following speech:

MR. CHAIRMAN, I am reminded by the oc-
currences of this afternoon of two characters
in the war of the Revolution as compared with
two others in the war of to-day.

The first was Lord Fairfax, who dwelt near
the Potomac, a few miles from us. When the
great contest was opened between the mother
country and the colonies, Lord Fairfax, after
a protracted struggle with his own heart, decided he must go with the mother country. He
gathered his mantle about him and went over
grandly and solemnly.

There was another man, who cast in his lot
with the struggling colonists, and continued
with them till the war was well-nigh ended.
In an hour of darkness that just preceded the
glory of the morning, he hatched the treason
to surrender forever all that had been gained
to the enemies of his country. Benedict Arnold
was that man!

Fairfax and Arnold find their parallels of
to-day.

When this war began many good men
stood hesitating and doubting what they

ought to do. Robert E. Lee sat in his house across the river here, doubting and delaying, and going off at last almost tearfully to join the army of his State. He reminds one in some respects of Lord Fairfax, the stately Royalist of the Revolution.

But now when tens of thousands of brave souls have gone up to God under the shadow of the flag; when thousands more, maimed and shattered in the contest, are sadly awaiting the deliverance of death; now, when three years of terrific warfare have raged over us; when our armies have pushed the Rebellion back over mountains and rivers, and crowded it into narrow limits, until a wall of fire girds it; now when the uplifted hand of a majestic people is about to hurl the bolts of its conquering power upon the Rebellion; now, in the quiet of this hall, hatched in the lowest depths of a similar dark treason, there rises a Benedict Arnold, and proposes to surrender all up, body and spirit, the nation and the flag, its genius and its honor, now and forever, to the accursed traitors to our country! And that proposition comes—God forgive and pity our beloved State—it comes from a citizen of the time-honored and loyal commonwealth of Ohio!

I implore you, brethren in this House, to believe that not many births ever gave pangs to my mother State such as she suffered when that traitor was born! I beg you not to believe that on the soil of that State another such a growth has ever deformed the face of nature, and darkened the light of God's day!

CHAPTER XXVII.
GARFIELD'S COURSE IN CONGRESS.

If Garfield at once took a prominent place in the House of Representatives, it was by no means because it was composed of inferior men. On the other hand, there has seldom been a time when it contained a larger number of men either prominent, or destined in after days to be prominent. I avail myself of the detailed account given of its members by Major Bundy, in his excellent *Life of Garfield*. There are some names which will be familiar to most of my young readers:

Its then most fortunate and promising member was Schuyler Colfax, the popular Speaker. But there were three young members who were destined to a more lasting prominence. The senior of these who had enjoyed previous service in he House, was Roscoe Conkling, already recognized by Congress and the country as a magnificent and convincing speaker. The other two were James G. Blaine and James A. Garfield. Only a year the senior of Garfield, Blaine was about to begin a career as brilliant as that of Henry Clay, and the acquisition of a popularity unique in our political history. But in this Congress there were many members whose power was far greater than that of either of the trio, who may yet be as much compared as Clay, Webster, and Calhoun were in former days.

In the first place, there was Elihu B. Washburne, "the watch-dog of the treasury," the "father of the House," courageous, practical, direct, and aggressive. Then there was Thaddeus Stevens, who was one of the very few men capable of driving his party associates—a character as unique as, and far stronger than, John Randolph; General Robert C. Schenck, fresh from the army, but a veteran in Congress, one of the ablest of practical statesmen; ex-Governor Boutwell, of Massachusetts; ex-Governor Fenton, of New York, a very influential member, especially on financial questions; Henry Winter Davis, the brilliant orator, of Maryland; William B. Allison, since one of the soundest and most useful of Iowa's Senators; Henry L. Dawes, who fairly earned his promotion to the Senate, but who accomplished so much in the House that his best friends regret the transfer; John A. Bingham, one of the most famous speakers of his time; James E. English, of Connecticut, who did valiant and patriotic service as a War Democrat; George H. Pendleton, now Senator from Ohio, and a most accomplished statesman, even in his early service in the House; Henry G. Stebbins, who was to make a speech sustaining Mr. Chase's financial policy that was unequaled for its salutary effect on public opinion; Samuel J. Randall, now Speaker; John A. Griswold, of New York; William Windom, one of the silent

members, who has grown steadily in power;
James F. Wilson, who was destined to decline
three successive offers of Cabinet positions
by President Grant; Daniel W. Voorhies, of
Indiana, now Senator; John A. Kasson, of
Iowa, now our Minister to Austria; Theodore
M. Pomeroy, of New York, afterward Acting
Speaker for a brief period; William R. Morri-
son, of Illinois, since a Democratic candidate
for the Presidency; William S. Holman and
George W. Julian, of Indiana, both able men;
and Fernando Wood—these were all prominent members of the House. It will be seen
that the House was a more trying arena for
a young member like Garfield than the Senate would have been; for the contests of the
former—unsubdued and unmitigated by "the
courtesy of the Senate"—were conducted by
as ready and able a corps of debaters as ever
sat in that body.

This was surely a formidable array of men,
and a man of ordinary powers would have found
it prudent to remain silent during the first session, lest he should be overwhelmed by some one
of the ready speakers and experienced legislators
with whom he was associated. But the canal-boy,
who had so swiftly risen from his humble position
to the post of college president and major-general, till at the age of thirty-two he sat in the national council the youngest member, was not daunted.
His term of service as State Senator was now of
use to him, for it had given him a knowledge of

parliamentary law, and the practice in speaking which he gained long ago in the boys' debating societies, and extended in college, rendered him easy and master of himself.

Indeed he could not remain silent, for he represented the "boys at the front," and whenever a measure was proposed affecting their interests, he was expected to take part in the debate. It was not long before the House found that its new member was a man of grace and power, with whom it was not always safe to measure weapons. He was inclined to be peaceful, but he was not willing to permit any one to domineer over him, and the same member did not often attempt it a second time.

My young readers are sure to admire pluck, and they will, therefore, read with interest of one such occasion, when Garfield effectually quelled such an attempt. I find it in a chapter of reminiscences contributed to the Boston *Journal*, by Ben Perley Poore, the well-known correspondent:

When the Jenckes Bankrupt Bill came before the House, Gen. Garfield objected to it, because in his opinion it did not provide that the estates of rebels in arms should escape the operations of the law. He also showed that money was being raised to secure the enactment of the bill, and Mr. Spalding, of the Cleveland district, was prompted by Mr. Jenckes to "sit down on him." But Gen. Garfield was not to be silenced easily and quite a scene ensued. The next day Garfield rose to a personal explanation, and said:

"I made no personal reference whatever; I assailed no gentleman; I called no man's honor in question. My colleague from the Cleveland district (Mr. Spalding) rose and asked if I had read the bill. I answered him, I believe, in courteous language and manner, that I had read it, and immediately on my statement to that effect he said in his place in the House, and it has gone on the record, that he did not believe I had read it; in other words, that he believed I had lied, in the presence of my peers in this House. I felt, under such circumstances, that it would not be becoming my self-respect, or the respect I owe to the House, to continue a colloquy with any gentleman who had thus impeached my veracity and I said so.

"It pains me very much that a gentleman of venerable age, who was in full maturity of life when I was a child, and whom I have respected since my childhood, should have taken occasion here in this place to use language so uncalled for, so ungenerous, so unjust to me, and disgraceful to himself. I have borne with the ill-nature and bad blood of that gentleman, as many others in this House have, out of respect for his years; but no importunity of age shall shield him, or any man, from my denunciation, who is so lacking in the proprieties of this place as to be guilty of such parliamentary and personal indecency as the House has witnessed on his part. I had hoped that before this time he would have acknowledged to me the impropriety and unjustifiableness of his conduct and apologized for the insult. But he has not seen fit to take this course. I leave him to his own reflections, and his conduct to the judgment of the House."

Those who listened to these spirited rebukes saw that the young member from Ohio would not allow himself to be snubbed or insulted with impunity, and the few who were accustomed to descend to such discourtesy took warning accordingly. They were satisfied that Garfield, to quote a common phrase, would give them as good as they sent, and perhaps a little better. The boy, who at sixteen, when employed on the towpath, thrashed the bully of thirty-five for insulting him, was not likely in his manhood to submit to the insults of a Congressional bully. He was a man to compel respect, and had that resolute and persistent character which was likely ere long to make him a leader. So Disraeli, coughed down in his first attempt to speak before the English House of Commons, accepted the situation, but recorded the prediction that one day they would hear him. He, too, mounted step by step till he reached the highest position in the English Government outside of royalty. A man who is destined to be great is only strengthened by opposition, and rises in the end victorious over circumstances.

Garfield soon made it manifest that he had come to Washington to work. He was not one to lie back and enjoy in idleness the personal consequence which his position gave him. All his life he had been a worker, and a hard worker, from the time when he cut one hundred cords of wood, at twenty-five cents a cord, all through his experience as a canal-boy, a carpenter, a farm-worker, a janitor, a school teacher, a student, and a military commander, and now that he had taken his place in the grand council of the nation, he was not going to begin a life of self-indulgent idleness.

In consideration of his military record he was, at his entrance into Congress, put upon the Military Committee; but a session or two later, at his own request, he was assigned a place on the Committee of Ways and Means. His reason for this request was, that he might have an opportunity of studying the question of finance, which he had sufficient foresight to perceive would one day be a great question, overshadowing all others. He instantly set himself to a systematic and exhaustive study of this subject, and attained so thorough a knowledge of it that he was universally recognized as a high authority—perhaps the highest in the department. He made speech after speech on the finance question, and was a pronounced advocate of "Honest Money," setting his face like a flint against those who advocated any measures calculated to lower the national credit or tarnish the national reputation for good faith.

"I am aware," said he one day in debate, "that financial measures are dull and uninviting in comparison with those heroic themes which have absorbed the attention of Congress for the last five years. To turn from the consideration of armies and navies, victories and defeats, to the array of figures which exhibits the debt, expenditure, taxation, and industry of the nation requires no little courage and self-denial; but to these questions we must come, and to their solution Congress and all thoughtful citizens must give their best efforts for many years to come."

It was not only a wise but a bold thing to do, for among the members of his own party, in Ohio, financial heresies had crept in, and a party platform was adopted in 1867, looking to the payment of the bonds of the Government in greenbacks. He was advised to say nothing on the subject lest it should cost him the nomination in the election just at hand; but he met the question boldly, and declared that the district could only have his services "on the ground of the honest payment of this debt, and these bonds in coin, according to the letter and spirit of the contract."

Nevertheless he was renominated by acclamation.

CHAPTER XXVIII.
THE MAN FOR THE HOUR.

On the 15th day of April, 1865, the country was thrilled from end to end by the almost incredible report that President Lincoln had been assassinated the evening previous while witnessing a performance at Ford's Theatre, in Washington.

The war was not yet over, but peace seemed close at hand. All were anticipating its return with joy. The immense sacrifices of loyal men seemed about to be rewarded when, like a clap of thunder in a clear sky, came the terrible tidings, which were flashed at once over the telegraphic wires to the remotest parts of the country.

The people at first were shocked and silent. Then a mighty wave of wrath swept over the country—a wrath that demanded victims, and seemed likely in the principal city of the country to precipitate scenes not unlike those witnessed in the "Reign of Terror" in France.

The boys who read this story can not understand the excitement of that day. It was unlike the deep sorrow that came upon us all on the second of July, for Lincoln died a martyr, at a time when men's passions had been stirred by sectional strife, and his murder was felt to be an outgrowth of the passions which it engendered; but Garfield fell, slain by the hand of a worthless wretch, acting upon his own responsibility.

I shall venture, for the information of young readers, to whom it may be new, to quote the graphic description of an eye-witness, contributed to General Brisbin's interesting life of our subject:

I shall never forget the first time I saw General Garfield. It was the morning after President Lincoln's assassination. The country was excited to its utmost tension.... The newspaper head lines of the transaction were set up in the largest type, and the high crime was on every one's tongue. Fear took possession of men's minds as to the fate of the Government, for in a few hours the news came on that Seward's throat was cut, and that attempts had been made on the lives of others of the Government officers. Posters were stuck up everywhere, in great black letters, calling upon the loyal citizens of New York, Brooklyn, Jersey City, and neighboring places, to meet around the Wall Street Exchange and give expression to their sentiments.

It was a dark and terrible hour. What might come next no one could tell, and men spoke with bated breath. The wrath of the working-men was simply uncontrollable, and revolvers and knives were in the hands of thousands of Lincoln's friends, ready, at the first opportunity, to take the law into their own hands, and avenge the death of their martyred President upon any and all who dared to utter a word against him.

Eleven o'clock A.M. was the hour set for the rendezvous. Fifty thousand people crowded around the Exchange building, cramming and jamming the streets, and wedged in as tight as men could stand together. With a few to whom special favor was extended, I went over from Brooklyn at nine A.M., and even then, with the utmost difficulty, found my way to the reception room for the speakers in the front of the Exchange building, and looking out on the high and massive balcony, whose front was protected by a massive iron railing.

We sat in solemnity and silence, waiting for General Butler, who, it was announced, had started from Washington, and was either already in the city or expected every moment.

Nearly a hundred generals, judges, statesmen, lawyers, editors, clergymen, and others were in that room waiting for Butler's arrival.

We stepped out to the balcony to watch the fearfully solemn and swaying mass of people. Not a hurrah was heard, but for the most part a dead silence, or a deep, ominous muttering ran like a rising wave up the street toward Broadway, and again down toward the river on the right. At length the batons of the police were seen swinging in the air, far up on the left, parting the crowd, and pressing it back to make way for a carriage that moved slowly, and with difficult jags through the compact multitude, and the cry of "Butler!" "Butler!" rang out with tremendous and thrilling effect, and was taken up by the people.

But not a hurrah! Not one! It was the cry of a great people asking to know how their President died. The blood bounced in our veins, and the tears ran like streams down our faces. How it was done I forget, but Butler was pulled through, and pulled up, and entered the room where we had just walked back to meet him. A broad crape, a yard long, hung from his left arm—terrible contrast with the countless flags that were waving the nation's victory in the breeze. We first realized then the sad news that Lincoln was dead. When Butler entered the room we shook hands. Some spoke, some could not; all were in tears. The only word Butler had for us all, at the first break of the silence was, *"Gentleman, he died in the fullness of his fame!"* and as he spoke it his lips quivered, and the tears ran fast down his cheeks.

Then, after a few moments, came the speaking. And you can imagine the effect, as the crape fluttered in the wind while his arm was uplifted. Dickinson, of New York State, was fairly wild. The old man leaped over the iron railing of the balcony and stood on the very edge, overhanging the crowd, gesticulating in the most vehement manner, and almost bidding the crowd "burn up the rebel, seed, root, and branch," while a bystander held on to his coat-tail to keep him from falling over.

By this time the wave of popular indignation had swelled to its crest. Two men lay bleeding on one of the side streets, the one dead, the other next to dying; one on the pavement, the other in the gutter. They had said a moment before that "Lincoln ought to have been shot long ago!" They were not allowed to say it again. Soon two long pieces of scantling stood out above the heads of the crowd, crossed at the top like the letter X, and a looped halter pendant from the junction, a dozen men following its slow motion through the masses, while "Vengeance" was the cry.

On the right suddenly the shout arose, *"The World! The World!"* and a movement of perhaps eight thousand to ten thousand turning their faces in the direction of that building began to be executed.

It was a critical moment. What might come no one could tell, did that crowd get in front of that office; police and military would have availed little, or been too late. A telegram had just been read from Washington, "Seward is dying!" Just then, at that juncture, a man stepped forward with a small flag in his hand and beckoned to the crowd.

"Another telegram from Washington!"

And then, in the awful stillness of the crisis, taking advantage of the hesitation of the crowd, whose steps had been arrested a moment, a right arm was lifted skyward, and a voice, clear and steady, loud and distinct, spoke out:

"Fellow-citizens! Clouds and darkness are round about Him! His pavilion is dark waters, and thick clouds of the skies! Justice and judgment are the establishment of His throne! Mercy and truth shall go before His face! Fellow-citizens! God reigns and the Government at Washington still lives!"

The effect was tremendous. The crowd stood rooted to the ground with awe, gazing at the motionless orator, and thinking of God and the security of the Government in that hour. As the boiling waters subside and settle to the sea, when some strong wind beats it down, so the tumult of the people sank and became still. All took it as a divine omen. It was a triumph of eloquence, inspired by the moment, such as falls to but one man's lot, and that but once in a century. The genius of Webster, Choate, Everett, Seward, never reached it. What might have happened had the surging and maddened mob been let loose, none can tell. The man for the crisis was on the spot, more potent than Napoleon's guns at Paris. I inquired what was his name.

The answer came in a low whisper, "It is General Garfield, of Ohio."

It was a most dramatic scene, and a wonderful exhibition of the power of one man of intellect over a furious mob.

How, would the thrilling intensity of the moment have been increased, had some prophet, standing beside the inspired speaker, predicted that a little more than sixteen years later he who had calmed the crowd would himself fall a victim to violence, while filling the same high post as the martyred Lincoln. Well has it been said that the wildest dream of the romancer pales beside the solemn surprise of the Actual. Not one among the thousands there assembled, not the speaker himself, would have considered such a statement within the range of credibility. Alas, that it should have been!—that the monstrous murder of the good Lincoln should have been repeated in these latter days, and the nation have come a second time a mourner!

Will it be believed that Garfield's arrival and his speech had been quite accidental, though we must also count it as Providential, since it stayed the wild excesses of an infuriated mob. He had only arrived from Washington that morning, and after breakfast had strolled through the crowded streets, in entire ignorance of the great gathering at the Exchange building.

He turned down Broadway, and when he saw the great concourse of people, he kept on, to learn what had brought them together. Butler was speaking when he arrived, and a friend who recognized him beckoned him to come up there, above the heads of the multitude.

When he heard the wild cries for "Vengeance!" and noticed the swaying, impassioned movements of the crowd, he saw the danger that menaced the public order, and in a moment of inspiration he rose, and with a gesture challenged the attention of the crowd. What he said he could not have told five minutes afterward. "I only know," he said afterward, "that I drew the lightning from that crowd, and brought it back to reason."

CHAPTER XXIX.
GARFIELD AS A LAWYER.

In the crowded activities of Garfield's life, my readers may possibly have forgotten that he was a lawyer, having, after a course of private study during his presidency of Hiram College, been admitted to the bar, in 1861, by the Supreme Court of Ohio. When the war broke out he was about to withdraw from his position as teacher, and go into practice in Cleveland; but, as a Roman writer has expressed it, *Inter arma silent leges*. So law gave way to arms, and the incipient lawyer became a general.

When the soldier put off his armor it was to enter Congress, and instead of practicing law, Garfield helped to frame laws.

But in 1865 there came an extraordinary occasion, which led to the Ohio Congressman entering upon his long delayed profession. And here I quote from the work of Major Bundy, already referred to:

About that time that great lawyer, Judge Jeremiah S. Black, as the attorney of the Ohio Democrats who had been opposing the war, came to his friend Garfield, and said that there were some men imprisoned in Indiana for conspiracy against the Government in trying to prevent enlistments and to encourage desertion. They had been tried in 1864, while the war was going on, and by a military commission sitting in Indiana, where there was no war, they had been sentenced to death. Mr. Lincoln commuted the sentence to imprisonment for life, and they were put into State's prison in accordance with the commutation. They then took out a writ of *habeas corpus*, to test the constitutionality and legality of their trial, and the judges in the Circuit Court had disagreed, there being two of them, and had certified their disagreement to the Supreme Court of the United States. Judge Black said to Garfield that he had seen what Garfield had said in Congress, and asked him if he was willing to say in an argument in the Supreme Court what he had advocated in Congress.

To which Garfield replied: "It depends on your case altogether."

Judge Black sent him the facts in the case—the record.

"Garfield read it over, and said: 'I believe in that doctrine.'

To which Judge Black replied: "Young man, you know it is a perilous thing for a young Republican in Congress to say that, and I don't want you to injure yourself."

Said Garfield: "It does not make any difference. I believe in English liberty, and English law. But, Judge Black, I am not a practitioner in the Supreme Court, and I never tried a case in my life anywhere."

"How long ago were you admitted to the bar?" asked Judge Black.

"Just about six years ago."

"That will do," Black replied, and he took Garfield thereupon over to the Supreme Court and moved his admission.

He immediately entered upon the consideration of this important case. On the side of the Government was arrayed a formidable amount of legal talent. The Attorney-General was aided by Gen. Butler, who was called in on account of his military knowledge, and by Henry Stanbury. Associated with Gen. Garfield as counsel for the petitioners were two of the greatest lawyers in the country—Judge Black and Hon. David Dudley Field, and the Hon. John E. McDonald, now Senator from Indiana. The argument submitted by Gen.

Garfield was one of the most remarkable ever made before the Supreme Court of the United States, and was made under circumstances peculiarly creditable to Garfield's courage, independence, and resolute devotion to the cause of constitutional liberty—a devotion not inspired by wild dreams of political promotion, for at that time it was dangerous for any young Republican Congressman to defend the constitutional rights of men known to be disloyal, and rightly despised and hated for their disloyal practices.

I refer any of my maturer readers who may desire an abstract of the young lawyer's masterly and convincing argument, to Major Bundy's valuable work, which necessarily goes more deeply into such matters than the scope of my slighter work will admit. His argument was listened to with high approval by his distinguished associate counsel, and the decision of the Supreme Court was given unanimously in favor of his clients.

Surely this was a most valuable *début*, and Garfield is probably the first lawyer that ever tried his first case before that august tribunal. It was a triumph, and gave him an immediate reputation and insured him a series of important cases before the same court. I have seen it stated that he was employed in seventeen cases before the Supreme Court, some of large importance, and bringing him in large fees. But for his first case he never received a cent. His clients were poor and in prison, and he was even obliged to pay for printing his own brief. His future earnings from this source, however, added materially to his income, and enabled him to install his family in that cherished home at Mentor, which has become, so familiar by name to the American people.

I can not dwell upon Garfield's experience as a lawyer. I content myself with quoting, from a letter addressed by Garfield to his close friend, President Hinsdale, of Hiram College, the account of a case tried in Mobile, which illustrates his wonderful industry and remarkable resources.

Under date of June 18, 1877, Garfield writes:

You know that my life has abounded in crises and difficult situations. This trip has been, perhaps, not a crisis, but certainly has placed me in a position of extreme difficulty. Two or three months ago, W.B. Duncan, a prominent business man in New York, retained me as his lawyer in a suit to be heard in the United States Court in Mobile, and sent me the papers in the case. I studied them, and found that they involved an important and somewhat difficult question of law, and I made myself sufficiently familiar with it, so that when Duncan telegraphed me to be in Mobile on the first Monday in June, I went with a pretty comfortable sense of my readiness to meet anybody who should be employed on the other side. But when I reached Mobile, I found there were two other suits connected with this, and involving the ownership, sale, and complicated rights of several parties to the Mobile and Ohio Railroad.

After two days' skirmishing, the court ordered the three suits to be consolidated. The question I had prepared myself on passed wholly out of sight, and the whole entanglement of an insolvent railroad, twenty-five years old, and lying across four States, and costing $20,000,000, came upon us at once. There were seven lawyers in the case besides me. On one side were John A. Campbell, of New Orleans, late member of the Supreme Bench of the United States; a leading New York and a Mobile lawyer. Against us were Judge Hoadley, of Cincinnati, and several Southern men. I was assigned the duty of summing up the case for our side, and answering the final argument of the opposition. I have never felt myself in such danger of failure before, all had so much better knowledge of the facts than I, and all had more experience with that class of litigation; but I am very sure no one of them did so much hard work, in the five nights and six days of the trial, as I did. I am glad to tell you that I have received a dispatch from Mobile, that the court adopted my view of the case, and gave us a verdict on all points.

Who can doubt, after reading of these two cases, that had Garfield devoted himself to the practice of the law exclusively, he would have made one of the most successful members of the profession in the country, perhaps risen to the highest rank? As it was, he was only able to devote the time he could spare from his legislative labors.

These increased as years sped. On the retirement of James G. Blaine from the lower House of Congress, the leadership of his party devolved upon Garfield. It was a post of honor, but it imposed upon him a vast amount of labor. He must qualify himself to speak, not superficially, but from adequate knowledge upon all points of legislation, and to defend the party with which he was allied from all attacks of political opponents.

On this subject he writes, April 21, 1880:

The position I hold in the House requires an enormous amount of surplus work. I am compelled to look ahead at questions likely to be sprung upon us for action, and the fact is, I prepare for debate on ten subjects where I actually take part in but one. For example, it seemed certain that the Fitz John Porter case would be discussed in the House, and I devoted the best of two weeks to a careful "re-examination" of the old material, and a study of the new.

There is now lying on top of my book-case a pile of books, revisions, and manuscripts, three feet long by a foot and a half high, which I accumulated and examined for debate, which certainly will not come off this session, perhaps not at all. I must stand in the breach to meet whatever comes.

I look forward to the Senate as at least a temporary relief from this heavy work. I am just now in antagonism with my own party on legislation in reference to the election law, and here also I have prepared for two discussions, and as yet have not spoken on either.

My young readers will see that Garfield thoroughly believed in hard work, and appreciated its necessity. It was the only way in which he could hold his commanding position. If he attained large success, and reached the highest dignity in the power of his countrymen to bestow, it is clear that he earned it richly. Upon some, accident bestows rank; but not so with him. From his earliest years he was growing, rounding out, and developing, till he became the man he was. And had his life been spared to the usual span, it is not likely that he would have desisted, but ripened with years into perhaps the most profound and scholarly statesman the world has seen.

CHAPTER XXX.
THE SCHOLAR IN POLITICS.

In the midst of his political and professional activity, Garfield never forgot his days of tranquil enjoyment at Hiram College, when he was devoted solely to the cultivation of his mind, and the extension of his knowledge. He still cherished the same tastes, and so far as his leisure—he had no leisure, save time snatched from the engrossing claims of politics—so far, at any rate, as he could manage the time, he employed it for new acquisitions, or for the review of his earlier studies.

In January, 1874, he made a metrical version

of the third ode of Horace's first book. I quote
four stanzas:

> Guide thee, O ship, on thy journey, that owest
> To Africa's shores Virgil trusted to thee.
> I pray thee restore him, in safety restore him,
> And saving him, save me the half of my soul.
>
> Stout oak and brass triple surrounded his bosom
> Who first to the waves of the merciless sea
> Committed his frail bark. He feared not Africa's
> Fierce battling the gales of the furious North.
>
> Nor feared he the gloom of the rain-bearing Hyads,
> Nor the rage of fierce Notus, a tyrant than whom
> No storm-god that rules o'er the broad Adriatic
> Is mightier its billows to rouse or to calm.
>
> What form, or what pathway of death him affrighted
> Who faced with dry eyes monsters swimming
>   the deep,
> Who gazed without fear on the storm-swollen billows,
> And the lightning-scarred rocks, grim with death
>   on the shore?

In reviewing the work of the year 1874, he
writes:

So far as individual work is concerned, I have
done something to keep alive my tastes and
habits. For example, since I left you I have
made a somewhat thorough study of Goethe
and his epoch, and have sought to build up in

my mind a picture of the state of literature and art in Europe, at the period when Goethe began to work, and the state when he died. I have grouped the various poets into order, so as to preserve memoirs of the impression made upon my mind by the whole. The sketch covers nearly sixty pages of manuscript. I think some work of this kind, outside the track of one's every-day work, is necessary to keep up real growth.

In July, 1875, he gives a list of works that he had read recently. Among these are several plays of Shakespeare, seven volumes of Froude's *England*, and a portion of Green's *History of the English People*. He did not limit himself to English studies, but entered the realms of French and German literature, having made himself acquainted with both these languages. He made large and constant use of the Library of Congress. Probably none of his political associates made as much, with the exception of Charles Sumner.

Major Bundy gives some interesting details as to his method of work, which I quote:

In all his official, professional, and literary work, Garfield has pursued a system that has enabled him to accumulate, on a vast range and variety of subjects, an amount of easily available information such as no one else has shown the possession of by its use. His house at Washington is a workshop, in which the tools are always kept within immediate reach.

Although books overrun his house from top to bottom, his library contains the working material on which he mainly depends. And the amount of material is enormous. Large numbers of scrap-books that have been accumulating for over twenty years, in number and in value—made up with an eye to what either is, or may become, useful, which would render the collection of priceless value to the library of any first-class newspaper establishment—are so perfectly arranged and indexed, that their owner with his all-retentive memory, can turn in a moment to the facts that may be needed for almost any conceivable emergency in debate.

These are supplemented by diaries that preserve Garfield's multifarous political, scientific, literary, and religious inquiries, studies, and readings. And, to make the machinery of rapid work complete, he has a large box containing sixty-three different drawers, each properly labeled, in which he places newspaper cuttings, documents, and slips of paper, and from which he can pull out what he wants as easily as an organist can play on the stops of his instrument. In other words, the hardest and most masterful worker in Congress has had the largest and most scientifically arranged of workshops.

It was a pleasant house, this, which Garfield had made for himself in Washington. With a devoted wife, who sympathized with him in his

literary tastes, and aided him in his preparation
for his literary work, with five children (two
boys now at Williams College, one daughter,
and two younger sons), all bright and promising, with a happy and joyous temperament that
drew around him warmly-attached friends, with
a mind continually broadening and expanding in
every direction, respected and appreciated by his
countrymen, and loved even by his political opponents, Garfield's lot seemed and was a rarely
happy one. He worked hard, but he had always
enjoyed work. Higher honors seemed hovering in
the air, but he did not make himself anxious about
them. He enjoyed life, and did his duty as he went
along, ready to undertake new responsibilities
whenever they came, but by no means impatient
for higher honors.

Filling an honored place in the household is
the white-haired mother, who, with justifiable
pride, has followed the fortunes of her son from
his destitute boyhood, along the years in which
he gained strength by battling with poverty and
adverse circumstances, to the time when he fills
the leading place in the councils of the nation. So
steadily has he gone on, step by step, that she is
justified in hoping for him higher honors.

The time came, and he was elected to the
United States Senate in place of Judge Thurman,
who had ably represented the State in the same
body, and had been long regarded as one of the
foremost leaders of the Democratic party. But
his mantle fell upon no unworthy successor. Ohio
was fortunate in possessing two such men to rep-

resent her in the highest legislative body of the nation.

Doubtless this honor would have come sooner to Garfield, for in 1877 he was the candidate to whom all eyes were directed, but he could not be spared from the lower House, there being no one to take his place as leader. He yielded to the expressed wishes of President Hayes, who, in the exceptional position in which he found himself, felt the need of a strong and able man in the House, to sustain his administration and help carry out the policy of the Government. Accustomed to yield his own interest to what he regarded as the needs of his country, Garfield quietly acquiesced in what to most men would have been a severe disappointment.

But when, after the delay of four years, he was elected to the Senate, he accepted with a feeling of satisfaction—not so much because he was promoted as because, in his new sphere of usefulness, he would have more time for the gratification of his literary tastes.

In a speech thanking the members of the General Assembly for their support, he said:

And now, gentlemen of the General Assembly, without distinction of party, I recognize this tribute and compliment paid to me tonight. Whatever my own course may be in the future, a large share of the inspiration of my future public life will be drawn from this occasion and from these surroundings, and I shall feel anew the sense of obligation that I feel to the State of Ohio. Let me venture to point a single sentence in regard to that work. During the twenty years that I have been in public life, almost eighteen of it in the Congress of the United States, I have tried to do one thing. Whether I was mistaken or otherwise, it has been the plan of my life to follow my conviction at whatever cost to myself.

I have represented for many years a district in Congress whose approbation I greatly desired; but, though it may seem, perhaps, a little egotistical to say it, I yet desired still more the approbation of one person, and his name was Garfield. [*Laughter and applause*]. He is the only man that I am compelled to sleep with, and eat with, and live with, and die with; and, if I could not have his approbation, I should have had companionship. [*Renewed laughter and applause*]. And in this larger constituency which has called me to represent them now, I can only do what is true to my best self, following the same rule. And if I should be so unfortunate as to lose the confidence of this larger constituency, I must do what every other fair-minded man has to do—carry his political life in his hand and take the consequences. But I must follow what seems to me to be the only safe rule of my life; and with that view of the case, and with that much personal reference, I leave that subject.

This speech gives the key-note of Garfield's political action. More than once he endangered his re-election and hazarded his political future by running counter to what he knew to be the wishes of his constituents and his party; but he would never allow himself to be a slave to party, or wear the yoke of political expediency. He sought, first of all, to win the approval of his own conscience and his own sense of right, and then he was willing to "take the consequences," even if they were serious enough to cut short the brilliant career which he so much enjoyed.

I conceive that in this respect he was a model whom I may safely hold up for the imitation of my readers, young or old. Such men do credit to the country, and if Garfield's rule of life could be universally adopted, the country would never be in peril. A conscientious man may make mistakes of judgment but he can never go far astray.

CHAPTER XXXI.
THE TRIBUTES OF FRIENDS.

Before going farther, in order that my young readers may be better qualified to understand what manner of man Garfield was, I will quote the remarks made by two of his friends, one a prominent member of the party opposed to him in politics. In the Milwaukee *Sentinel* of Sept. 22d, I find this tribute by Congressman Williams, of that State:

Happening to sit within one seat of him for four years in the House, I, with others, perhaps had a better opportunity to see him in all of his moods than those more removed. In action he was a giant; off duty he was a great, noble boy. He never knew what austerity of manner or ceremonious dignity meant. After some of his greatest efforts in the House, such as will live in history, he would turn to me, or any one else, and say: "Well, old boy, how was that?" Every man was his confidant and friend, so far as the interchange of every-day good feeling was concerned.

He once told me how he prepared his speeches; that first he filled himself with the subject, massing all the facts and principles involved, so far as he could; then he took pen and paper and wrote down the salient points in what he regarded their logical order. Then he scanned them critically, and fixed them in his memory. "And then," said he, "I leave the paper in my room and trust to the emergency." He told me that when he spoke at the serenade in New York a year ago, he was so pressed by callers that the only opportunity he had for preparation was, to lock the door and walk three times around the table, when he was called out to the balcony to begin. All the world knows what that speech was.

He was wrapped up in his family. His two boys would come up to the House just before adjournment, and loiter about his desk with their books in their hands. After the House adjourned, other members would go off in cars or carriages, or walk down the avenue in groups. But Garfield, with a boy on each side of him, would walk down Capitol Hill, as we would say in the country "cross-lots," all three chatting together on equal terms.

He said to me one day during the canvass, while the tears came to his eyes, "I have done no more in coming up from poverty than hundreds and thousands of others, but I am thankful that I have been able to keep my family by my side, and educate my children."

He was a man with whom anybody could differ with impunity. I have said repeatedly, that were Garfield alive and fully recovered, and a dozen of his intimate friends were to go to him, and advise that Guiteau be let off, he would say, "Yes, let him go." The man positively knew no malice. And for such a man to be shot and tortured like a dog, and by a dog!

He was extremely sensitive. I have seen him come into the House in the morning, when some guerrilla of the press had stabbed him deeper in his feelings than Guiteau's bullet did in the body, and when he looked pallid from suffering, and the evident loss of sleep; but he would utter no murmur, and in some short time his great exuberance of spirits would surmount it all, and he would be a boy again.

He never went to lunch without a troop of friends with him. He loved to talk at table, and there is no gush in saying he talked a God socially and intellectually. Some of his off-hand expressions were like a burst of inspiration. Like all truly great men, he did not seem to realize his greatness. And, as I have said, he would talk as cordially and confidentially with a child as with a monarch. And I only refer to his conversations with me because you ask me to, and because I think his off-hand conversations with any one reveal his real traits best.

Coming on the train from Washington, after his nomination, he said: "Only think of this! I am yet a young man; if elected and I serve my term I shall still be a young man. Then what am I going to do? There seems to be no place in America for an ex-President."

And then came in what I thought the extreme simplicity and real nobility of the man. "Why," said he, "I had no thought of being nominated. I had bought me some new books, and was getting ready for the Senate."

I laughed at the idea of his buying books, like a boy going to college, and remembered that during his Congressional career he had furnished materials for a few books himself. And then, with that peculiar roll of the body and slap on the shoulder with the left hand, which all will recognize, he said: "Why! do you know that up to 1856 I never saw a *Congressional Globe*, nor knew what one was!" And he then explained how he stumbled upon one in the hands of an opponent in his first public anti-slavery debate.

A friend remarked the other day that Garfield would get as enthusiastic in digging a six-foot ditch with his own hands, as when making a speech in Congress. Such was my observation. Going down the lane, he seemed to forget for the time that there was any Pres-

idential canvass pending. He would refer, first
to one thing, then another, with that off-hand
originality which was his great characteristic.
Suddenly picking up a smooth, round pebble,
he said, "Look at that! Every stone here sings
of the sea."

Asking why he bought his farm, he said
he had been reading about metals, how you
could draw them to a certain point a million
times and not impair their strength, but if you
passed that point once, you could never get
them back. "So," said he, "I bought this farm
to rest the muscles of my mind!" Coming to
two small wooden structures in the field, he
talked rapidly of how his neighbors guessed
he would do in Congress, but would not make
much of a fist at farming, and then called my
attention to his corn and buckwheat and other
crops, and said that was a marsh, but he un-
derdrained it with tile, and found spring-wa-
ter flowing out of the bluff, and found he could
get a five-foot fall, and with pumps of a given
dimension, a water-dam could throw water
back eighty rods to his house, and eighty feet
above it. "But," said he, in his jocularly, impressive manner, "I did my surveying before
I did my work."

This is certainly a pleasant picture of a great
man, who has not lost his simplicity of manner,
and who seems unconscious of his greatness—in
whom the love of humanity is so strong that he
reaches out a cordial hand to all of his kind, no

matter how humble, and shows the warmest interest in all.

Senator Voorhees, of Indiana, was among the speakers at the memorial meeting in Terre Haute, and in the course of his remarks, said:

I knew James A. Garfield well, and, except on the political field, we had strong sympathies together. It is nearly eighteen years since we first met, and during that period I had the honor to serve seven years in the House of Representatives with him.

The kindness of his nature and his mental activity were his leading traits. In all his intercourse with men, women, and children, no kinder heart ever beat in human breast than that which struggled on till 10.30 o'clock Monday night, and then forever stood still. There was a light in his face, a chord in his voice, and a pressure in his hand, which were full of love for his fellow-beings. His manners were ardent and demonstrative with those to whom he was attached, and he filled the private circle with sunshine and magnetic currents. He had the joyous spirits of boyhood and the robust intellectuality of manhood more perfectly combined than any other I ever knew. Such a character was necessarily almost irresistible with those who knew him personally, and it accounts for that undying hold which, under all circumstances, bound his immediate constituents to him as with hooks of steel. Such a nature, however, always has its dangers as well as its strength and its blessings. The kind heart and the open hand never accompany a suspicious, distrustful mind. Designing men mark such a character for their own selfishness, and Gen. Garfield's faults—for he had faults, as he was human—sprang more from this circumstance than from all others combined. He was prompt and eager to respond to the wishes of those he esteemed his friends, whether inside or outside of his own political party. That he made some mistakes in his long, busy career is but repeating the history of every generous and obliging man who has lived and died in public life. They are not such, however, as are recorded in heaven, nor will they mar or weaken the love of his countrymen.

The poor, laboring boy, the self-made man, the hopeful, buoyant soul in the face of all difficulties and odds, *constitute an example for the American youth, which will never be lost nor grow dim.*

The estimate to be placed on the intellectual abilities of Gen. Garfield must be a very high one. Nature was bountiful to him, and his acquirements were extensive and solid. If I might make a comparison, I would say that, with the exception of Jefferson and John Quincy Adams, he was the most learned President in what is written in books in the whole range of American history.

The Christian character of Gen. Garfield can not, with propriety, be omitted in a glance, however brief, at his remarkable career. Those who knew him best in the midst of his ambition and his worldly hopes will not fail now at his tomb to bear their testimony to his faith in God and his love for the teachings of the blessed Nazarene.

It seems but yesterday that I saw him last, and parted from him in all the glory of his physical and mental manhood. His eye was full of light, his tread elastic and strong, and the world lay bright before him. He talked freely of public men and public affairs. His resentments were like sparks from the flint. He cherished them not for a moment. Speaking of one who, he thought, had wronged him, he said to me, that, sooner or later, he intended to pour coals of fire on his head by acts of kindness to some of his kindred. He did not live to do so, but the purpose of his heart has been placed to his credit in the book of eternal life.

A correspondent of the New York *Tribune* suggests that the following lines, from Pollok's "Course of Time," apply with remarkable fitness to his glorious career:

Illustrious, too, that morning stood the man
Exalted by the people to the throne
Of government, established on the base
Of justice, liberty, and equal right;
Who, in his countenance sublime, expressed
A nation's majesty, and yet was meek
And humble; and in royal palace gave
Example to the meanest, of the fear

Of God, and all integrity of life
And manners; who, august, yet lowly; who
Severe, yet gracious; in his very heart
Detesting all oppression, all intent
Of private aggrandizement; and the first
In every public duty—held the scales
Of justice, and as law, which reigned in him,
Commanded, gave rewards; or with the edge
Vindictive smote—now light, now heavily,
According to the stature of the crime.
Conspicuous, like an oak of healthiest bough,
Deep-rooted in his country's love, he stood.

CHAPTER XXXII.
FROM CANAL-BOY TO PRESIDENT.

James A. Garfield had been elected to the United States Senate, but he was never a member of that body. Before the time came for him to take his seat he had been invested with a higher dignity. Never before in our history has the same man been an actual member of the House of Representatives, a Senator-elect, and President-elect.

On the 8th of June, 1880, the Republican Convention at Chicago selected Garfield as their standard-bearer on the thirty-sixth ballot. No one, probably, was more surprised or bewildered than Garfield himself, who was a member of the Convention, when State after State declared in his favor. In his loyalty to John Sherman, of his own State, whom he had set in nomination in an eloquent speech, he tried to avert the result, but in vain. He was known by the friends of other candidates to be thoroughly equipped for the highest office in the people's gift, and he was the second choice of the majority.

Mary Clemmer, the brilliant Washington correspondent, writes of the scene thus:

For days before, many that would not confess it felt that he was the coming man, because of the acclaim of the people whenever Garfield appeared. The culminating moment came. Other names seemed to sail out of sight like thistledown on the wind, till one (how glowing and living it was) was caught by the galleries, and shout on shout arose with the accumulative force of ascending breakers, till the vast amphitheater was deluged with sounding and resounding acclaim, such as a man could hope would envelope and uplift his name but once in a life-time. And he? There he stood, strong, Saxon, fair, debonair, yet white as new snow, and trembling like an aspen. It seemed too much, this sudden storm of applause and enthusiasm for him, the new idol, the coming President; yet who may say that through his exultant, yet trembling heart, that moment shot the presaging pang of distant, yet sure-coming woe?

Senator Hoar of Massachusetts, who was the President of the Convention, in a speech made not long afterward, paid the following just tribute to Garfield's character and qualifications:

Think of the qualifications for the office which that man combines. Do you want a statesman in the broadest sense? Do you demand a successful soldier? Do you want a man of more experience in civil affairs? No President of the United States since John Quincy Adams has begun to bring to the Presidential office, when he entered, anything like the experience in statesmanship of Gen. Garfield. As you look over the list, Grant, Jackson, and Taylor have brought to the position great fame as soldiers, but who since John Quincy Adams has had such a civil career to look back upon as Gen. Garfield? Since 1864 I can not think of one important question debated in Congress or discussed before the great tribunal of the American people in which you can not find the issue stated more clearly and better than by any one else in the speeches in the House of Representatives or on the hustings of Gen. Garfield—firm and resolute, constant in his adherence to what he thinks is right, regardless of popular delusions or the fear that he will become less popular, or be disappointed in his ambitions.

Just remember when Republicans and Democrats alike of Ohio fairly went crazy over the financial heresy, this man stood as with his feet on a rock, demanding honesty in government. About six years ago I sat by the side of an Ohio Representative, who had an elaborately prepared table, showing how the West was being cheated; that Ohio had not as many bank bills to the square mile as the East, and that the Southwest was even worse off than Ohio.

In regard to the great questions of human rights he has stood inflexible. The successor of Joshua R. Giddings, he is the man on whom his mantle may be said to have descended. Still he is no blind partisan. The best arguments in favor of civil service reform are found in the speeches of Gen. Garfield. He is liberal and generous in the treatment of the South, one of the foremost advocates of educational institutions in the South at the national expense. Do you wish for that highest type—the volunteer citizen soldier? Here is a man who enlisted at the beginning of the war; from a subordinate officer he became a major-general, trusted by those best of commanders, Thomas and Rosecranz, always in the thickest of the fight, the commander of dangerous and always successful expeditions, and returning home crowned with the laurels of victory. Do you wish for an honored career, which in itself is a vindication of the system of the American Republic? Without the attributes of rank or wealth, he has risen from the humblest to the loftiest position.

When the nominee of the convention had leisure to reflect upon his new position, and then cast his eye back along his past life, beginning with his rustic home in the Ohio wilderness, and traced step by step his progress from canal-boy to Presidential candidate, it must have seemed to him almost a dream. It was indeed a wonderful illustration of what we claim for our Republican institutions, the absolute right of the poorest and humblest, provided he has the requisite talent and industry to aspire to the chief place and the supreme power. "It was the most perfect instance of the resistless strength of a man developed by all the best and purest impulses, forces, and influences of American institutions into becoming their most thorough and ablest embodiment in organic and personal activity, aspiration, and character."

The response to the nomination throughout the country was most hearty. It was felt that the poor Ohio canal-boy had fitted himself, after an arduous struggle with poverty, for the high post to which he was likely to be called. The N.Y. *Tribune*, whose first choice had been the brilliant son of Maine, James G. Blaine, welcomed the result of the convention thus:

From one end of the nation to the other, from distant Oregon to Texas, from Maine to Arizona, lightning has informed the country of the nomination yesterday of James A. Garfield, as the Republican candidate for the Presidency.

Never was a nomination made which has been received by friend and foe with such evidence of hearty respect, admiration, and confidence. The applause is universal. Even the Democratic House of Representatives suspended its business that it might congratulate the country upon the nomination of the distinguished leader of the Republicans.

James Abram Garfield is, in the popular mind, one of the foremost statesmen of the nation. He is comparatively a young man, but in his service he commands the confidence and admiration of his countrymen of all parties. His ability, his thorough study, and his long practical experience in political matters gives an assurance to the country that he will carry to the Presidential office a mind superior, because of its natural qualifications and training, to any that has preceded him for many years. He will be a President worthy in every sense to fill the office in a way that the country will like to see it filled—with ability, learning, experience, and integrity. That Gen. Garfield will be elected we have no question. He is a candidate worthy of election, and will command not only every Republican vote in the country, but the support of tens of thousands of non-partisans who want to see a President combining intellectual ability with learning, experience, and ripe statesmanship.

The prediction recorded above was fulfilled. On the second of November, 1880, James A. Garfield was elected President of the United States.

Had this been a story of the imagination, such as I have often written, I should not have dared to crown it with such an ending. In view of my hero's humble beginnings, I should expect to have it severely criticised as utterly incredible, but reality is oftentimes stranger than romance, and this is notably illustrated in Garfield's wonderful career.

CHAPTER XXXIII.
THE NEW ADMINISTRATION.

On the evening of March 3d, preceding the inauguration, the President-elect met twenty of his college classmates at supper at Wormley's Hotel, in Washington, and mutual congratulations were exchanged. He was the first President of the United States selected from among the graduates of Williams College, and all the alumni, but more especially the class of 1856, were full of pride and rejoicing. From none probably were congratulations more welcome to the new President than from his old academic associates. If I transcribe the speech which Gen. Garfield made upon that occasion it is because it throws a light upon his character and interprets the feelings with which he entered upon the high office to which his countrymen had called him:

CLASSMATES: To me there is something exceedingly pathetic in this reunion. In every eye before me I see the light of friendship and love, and I am sure it is reflected back to each one of you from my inmost heart. For twenty-two years, with the exception of the last few days, I have been in the public service. To-night I am a private citizen. To-morrow

I shall be called to assume new responsibilities, and on the day after, the broadside of the world's wrath will strike. It will strike hard. I know it, and you will know it. Whatever may happen to me in the future, I shall feel that I can always fall back upon the shoulders and hearts of the class of '56 for their approval of that which is right, and for their charitable judgment wherein I may come short in the discharge of my public duties. You may write down in your books now the largest percentage of blunders which you think I will be likely to make, and you will be sure to find in the end that I have made more than you have calculated—many more.

This honor comes to me unsought. I have never had the Presidential fever—not even for a day; nor have I it to-night. I have no feeling of elation in view of the position I am called upon to fill. I would thank God were I to-day a free lance in the House or the Senate. But it is not to be, and I will go forward to meet the responsibilities and discharge the duties that are before me with all the firmness and ability I can command. I hope you will be able conscientiously to approve my conduct; and when I return to private life, I wish you to give me another class-meeting.

This brief address exhibits the modesty with which Gen. Garfield viewed his own qualifications for the high office for which twenty years of public life had been gradually preparing him.

While all are liable to mistakes, it is hardly to be supposed that a man so prepared, and inspired by a conscientious devotion to what he deemed to be right, would have made many serious blunders. During his brief administration he made, as the country knows, an admirable beginning in reforming abuses and exacting the most rigid economy in the public service. There was every probability of his being his own successor had his life been spared.

The inaugural ceremonies were very imposing. Washington was thronged as it had never been before on any similar occasion. Private citizens, civic bodies, and military companies were present from every part of the country. Prominent among the eminent citizens present was the stately and imposing figure of Gen. Hancock, who had been the nominee of the opposing party, and who, with admirable good feeling and good taste, had accepted an invitation to be present at the inauguration of his successful rival.

And there were others present whom we have met before. The wife and mother of the new President, with flushed cheeks and proud hearts, witnessed the ceremonies that made the one they loved the head of the State. To him they were more than all the rest. When he had taken the oath of office in the presence of the assembled tens of thousands, Garfield turned to his aged mother and imprinted a kiss upon her cheek, and afterward upon that of his wife. It was a touch of nature that appealed to the hearts of all present.

In the White House, one of the best rooms

was reserved for his aged mother, for whom he cherished the same fond love and reverence as in his boyish days. It was a change, and a great one, from the humble log-cabin in which our story opens; it was a change, too, from the backwoods boy, in his suit of homespun, to the statesman of noble and commanding figure, upon whom the eyes of the nation were turned. The boy who had guided the canal-boat was now at the helm of the national vessel, and there was no fear that he would run her aground. Even had storms come, we might safely trust in him who had steered the little steamboat up the Big Sandy River, in darkness and storm and floating obstructions, to the camp where his famished soldiers were waiting for supplies. For, as is the case with every great man, it was difficulty and danger that nerved Garfield to heroic efforts, and no emergency found him lacking.

His life must now be changed, and the change was not altogether agreeable. With his cordial off-hand manners, and Western freedom, he, no doubt, felt cramped and hampered by the requirements of his new position. When he expressed his preference for the position of a freelance in the House or Senate, he was sincere. It was more in accordance with his private tastes. But a public man can not always choose the place or the manner in which he will serve his country. Often she says to him, "Go up higher!" when he is content with an humble place, and more frequently, perhaps, he has to be satisfied with an humble place when he considers himself fitted for a higher.

So far as he could, Gen. Garfield tried to preserve in the Executive Mansion the domestic life
which he so highly prized. He had his children
around him. He made wise arrangements for
their continued education, for he felt that whatever other legacy he might be able to leave them,
this would be the most valuable. Still, as of old, he
could count on the assistance of his wife in fulfill-
ing the duties, social and otherwise, required by
his exalted position.

Nor was he less fortunate in his political
family. He had selected as his Premier a friend
and political associate of many years' standing,
whose brilliant talent and wide-spread reputation brought strength to his administration. In
accepting the tender of the post of Secretary of
State, Mr. Blaine said:

In our new relation I shall give all that I am,
and all that I can hope to be, freely and joyful-
ly to your service. You need no pledge of my
loyalty in heart and in act. I should be false to
myself did I not prove true both to the great
trust you confide to me, and to your own personal and political fortunes in the present and
in the future. Your administration must be
made brilliantly successful, and strong in the
confidence and pride of the people, not at all
directing its energies for re-election, and yet
compelling that result by the logic of events
and by the imperious necessities of the situation.

I accept it as one of the happiest circumstances connected with this affair, that in allying my political fortunes with yours—or rather, for the time merging mine in yours—my heart goes with my head, and that I carry to you not only political support, but personal and devoted friendship. I can but regard it as somewhat remarkable that two men of the same age, entering Congress at the same time, influenced by the same aims, and cherishing the same ambitions, should never, for a single moment, in eighteen years of close intimacy, have had a misunderstanding or a coolness, and that our friendship has steadily grown with our growth, and strengthened with our strength.

It is this fact which has led me to the conclusion embodied in this letter; for, however much, my dear Garfield, I might admire you as a statesman, I would not enter your Cabinet if I did not believe in you as a man and love you as a friend.

When it is remembered that Mr. Blaine before the meeting of the convention was looked upon as the probable recipient of the honor that fell to Garfield, the generous warmth of this letter will be accounted most creditable to both of the two friends, whose strong friendship rivalry could not weaken or diminish.

So the new Administration entered upon what promised to be a successful course. I can not help recording, as a singular circumstance, that the three highest officers were ex-teachers. Of Garfield's extended services as teacher, beginning with the charge of a district school in the wilderness, and ending with the presidency of a college, we already know. Reference has also been made to the early experience of the Vice-President, Chester A. Arthur, in managing a country school. To this it may be added that Mr. Blaine, too, early in life was a teacher in an academy, and, as may readily be supposed, a successful one. It is seldom in other countries that similar honors crown educational workers. It may be mentioned, however, that Louis Philippe, afterward King of the French, while an exile in this country, gave instruction in his native language. It is not, however, every ruler of boys that is qualified to become a ruler of men. Yet, in our own country, probably a majority of our public men have served in this capacity.

CHAPTER XXXIV.
THE TRAGIC END.

I should like to end my story here, and feel that it was complete. I should like with my countrymen to be still looking forward with interest to the successful results of an administration, guided by the experienced statesman whose career we have followed step by step from its humble beginnings. But it can not be.

On the second of July, in the present year, a startling rumor was borne on the wings of the lightning to the remotest parts of the land:

"President Garfield has been assassinated!"

The excitement was only paralleled by that

which prevailed in 1865, when Abraham Lincoln was treacherously killed by an assassin. But in this later case the astonishment was greater, and all men asked, "What can it mean?"

We were in a state of profound peace. No wars nor rumors of war disturbed the humble mind, and the blow was utterly unexpected and inexplicable.

The explanation came soon enough. It was the work of a wretched political adventurer, who, inflated by an overweening estimate of his own abilities and importance, had made a preposterous claim to two high political offices—the post of Minister to Austria, and Consul to Paris—and receiving no encouragement in either direction, had deliberately made up his mind to "remove" the President, as he termed it, in the foolish hope that his chances of gaining office would be better under another administration.

My youngest readers will remember the sad excitement of that eventful day. They will remember, also, how the public hopes strengthened or weakened with the varying bulletins of each day during the protracted sickness of the nation's head. They will not need to be reminded how intense was the anxiety everywhere manifested, without regard to party or section, for the recovery of the suffering ruler. And they will surely remember the imposing demonstrations of sorrow when the end was announced. Some of the warmest expressions of grief came from the South, who in this time of national calamity were at one with their brothers of the North. And

when, on the 26th of September, the last funeral
rites were celebrated, and the body of the dead
President was consigned to its last resting-place
in the beautiful Lake View Cemetery, in sight of
the pleasant lake on which his eyes rested as a
boy, never before had there been such imposing
demonstrations of grief in our cities and towns.

These were not confined to public buildings,
and to the houses and warehouses of the rich, but
the poorest families displayed their bit of crape.
Outside of a miserable shanty in Brooklyn was
displayed a cheap print of the President, framed
in black, with these words written below, "We
mourn our loss." Even as I write, the insignia of
grief are still to be seen in the tenement-house
districts on the East Side of New York, and there
seems a reluctance to remove them.

But not alone to our own country were confined the exhibitions of sympathy, and the anxious alternations of hope and fear. There was
scarcely a portion of the globe in which the hearts
of the people were not deeply stirred by the daily
bulletins that came from the sick couch of the patient sufferer. Of the profound impression made
in England I shall give a description, contributed
to the New York *Tribune* by its London correspondent, Mr. G.W. Smalley, only premising that
the sympathy and grief were universal: from
the Queen, whose messages of tender, womanly
sympathy will not soon be forgotten, to the humblest day-laborers in the country districts. Never
in England has such grief been exhibited at the
sickness and death of a foreign ruler, and the re-

membrance of it will draw yet closer together, for all time to come, the two great sections of the English-speaking tongue. Were it not a subject of such general interest, I should apologize for the space I propose to give to England's mourning:

It happened that some of the humbler classes were among the most eager to signify their feelings. The omnibus-drivers had each a knot of crape on his whip. Many of the cabmen had the same thing, and so had the draymen. In the city, properly so called, and along the water-side, it was the poorer shops and the smaller craft that most frequently exhibited tokens of public grief. Of the people one met in mourning the same thing was true. Between mourning put on for the day and that which was worn for private affliction it was not possible to distinguish. But in many cases it was plain enough that the black coat on the workingman's shoulders, or the bonnet or bit of crape which a shop-girl wore, was no part of their daily attire. They had done as much as they could to mark themselves as mourners for the President. It was not much, but it was enough. It had cost them some thought, a little pains, sometimes a little money, and they were people whose lives brought a burden to every hour, who had no superfluity of strength or means, and on whom even a slight effort imposed a distinct sacrifice. They are not of the class to whom the Queen's command for Court mourning was addressed. Few of that class are now in London. St. James' Street and Pall Mall, Belgravia and May Fair are depopulated. The compliance with the Queen's behest has been, I am sure, general and hearty, but evidences of it were to be sought elsewhere than in London.

Of other demonstrations it can hardly be necessary to repeat or enlarge upon the description you have already had. The drawn blinds of the Mansion House and of Buckingham Palace, the flags at half-mast in the Thames on ships of every nationality, the Stock and Metal Exchanges closed, the royal standard at half-mast on the steeple of the royal church of St. Martin-in-the-Fields; the darkened windows of great numbers of banking houses and other places of business in the city itself—of all these you have heard.

At the West End, the shops were not, as a rule, draped with black. Some of them had the Union Jack at half-mast; a few the Stars and Stripes in black with white and black hangings on the shop fronts. The greater number of shop-keepers testified to their association with the general feeling by shutters overhanging the tops of the windows, or by perpendicular slabs at intervals down the glass. Some had nothing; but in Regent Street, Bond Street, St. James' Street, and Piccadilly, which are the fashionable business streets of the West End, those which had nothing were the exception. The American Legation in Victoria Street, and the American Consulate in

Old Broad Street, both of which were closed, were in deep mourning. The American Dispatch Agency, occupying part of a conspicuous building in Trafalgar Square, had nothing to indicate its connection with America or any share in the general sorrow.

In many private houses—I should say the majority in such streets as I passed through during the day—the blinds were down as they would have been for a death in the family. The same is true of some of the clubs, and some of the hotels. The Reform Club, of which Garfield is said to have been an honorary member, had a draped American flag over the door.

To-day, as on every previous day since the President's death, the London papers print many columns of accounts, each account very brief, of what has been done and said in the so-called provincial towns. One journal prefaces its copious record by the impressive statement that from nearly every town and village telegraphic messages have been sent by its correspondents describing the respect paid to General Garfield on the day of his funeral. These tributes are necessarily in many places of a similar character, yet the variety of sources from which they proceed is wide enough to include almost every form of municipal, ecclesiastical, political, or individual activity. Everywhere bells are tolled, churches thrown open for service, flags drooping, business is interrupted, resolutions are passed. Liverpool, as is natural for the multiplicity and closeness of her relations with the United States, may perhaps be said to have taken the lead. She closed, either in whole or in part, her Cotton Market, her Produce Markets, her Provision Market, her Stock Exchange. Her papers came out in mourning. The bells tolled all day long.

Few merchants, one reads, came to their places of business, and most of those who came were in black. The Mayor and members of the Corporation, in their robes, attended a memorial service at St. Peter's, and the cathedral overflowed with its sorrowing congregation. Manchester, Newcastle, Birmingham, Glasgow, Bradford, Edinburgh were not much behind Liverpool in demonstrations, and not at all behind it in spirit. It is an evidence of the community of feeling between the two countries that so much of the action is official. What makes these official acts so striking, also, is the evident feeling at the bottom of this, that between England and America there is some kind of a relation which brings the loss of the President into the same category with the loss of an English ruler.

At Edinburgh it is the Lord Provost who orders the bells to be tolled till two. At Glasgow the Town Council adjourns. At Stratford-on-Avon the Mayor orders the flag to be hoisted at half-mast over the Town Hall, and the blinds to be drawn, and invites the citizens to follow his example, which they do; the bell at the Chapel of the Holy Cion tolling every minute while the funeral is solemnized at Cleveland. At Leeds the bell in the Town Hall is muffled and tolled, and the public meeting which the United States Consul, Mr. Dockery, addresses, is under the presidency of the acting Mayor. Mr. Dockery remarked that as compared with other great towns, so few were the American residents in Leeds, that the great exhibition of sympathy had utterly amazed him. The remark is natural, but Mr. Dockery need not have been amazed. The whole population of Leeds was American yesterday; and of all England. At Oxford the Town Council voted an address to Mrs. Garfield. At the Plymouth Guildhall the maces, the emblems of municipal authority, were covered with black. At Dublin the Lord Mayor proposed, and the Aldermen adopted, a resolution of sympathy.

In all the cathedral towns the cathedral authorities prescribed services for the occasion. I omit, because I have no room for them, scores of other accounts, not less significant and not less affecting. They are all in one tone and one spirit. Wherever in England, yesterday, two or three were gathered together, President Garfield's name was heard. Privately and publicly, simply as between man and man, or formally with the decorous solemnity and stately observance befitting bodies which bear a relation to the Government, a tribute of honest grief was offered to the President and his family, and of honest sympathy to his country. Steeple spoke to steeple, distant cities clasped hands. The State, the Church, the people of England were at one together in their sorrow, and in their earnest wish to offer some sort of comfort to their mourning brothers beyond the sea. You heard in every mouth the old cry, "Blood is thicker than water." And the voice which is perhaps best entitled to speak for the whole nation added, "Yes, though the water be a whole Atlantic Ocean."

In addition to these impressive demonstrations, the Archbishop of Canterbury held a service and delivered an address in the church of St. Martin-in-the-Fields, on Monday. Mr. Lowell had been invited, of course, by the church wardens, and a pew reserved for him, but when he reached the church with his party half his pew was occupied.

The Archbishop, who wore deep crape over his Episcopal robes, avoided calling his discourse a sermon, and avoided, likewise, through the larger portion of it, the purely professional tone common in the pulpit on such occasions. During a great part of his excellent address he spoke, as anybody else might have done, of the manly side of the President's character. He gave, moreover, his own view of the reason why all England has been so strangely moved. "During the long period of the President's suffering," said the Archbishop, "we had time to think what manner of man this was over whom so great a nation was mourning day by day. We learned what a noble history his was, and we were taught to trace a career such as England before knew nothing of."

"Among the innumerable testimonies to the purity and beauty of Garfield's character," says Mr. Smalley, "this address of the Primate of the English Church surely is one which all Americans may acknowledge with grateful pride."

CHAPTER XXXV.
MR. DEPEW'S ESTIMATE OF GARFIELD.

My task is drawing near a close. I have, in different parts of this volume, expressed my own estimate of our lamented President. No character in our history, as it seems to me, furnishes a brighter or more inspiring example to boys and young men. It is for this reason that I have been induced to write the story of his life especially for American boys, conceiving that in no way can I do them a greater service.

But I am glad, in confirmation of my own estimate, to quote at length the eloquent words of Hon. Chauncey M. Depew, in his address before the Grand Army of the Republic. He says of Garfield:

In America and Europe he is recognized as an illustrious example of the results of free institutions. His career shows what can be accomplished where all avenues are open and exertion is untrammeled. Our annals afford no such incentive to youth as does his life, and it will become one of the republic's household stories. No boy in poverty almost hopeless, thirsting for knowledge, meets an obstacle which Garfield did not experience and overcome. No youth despairing in darkness feels a gloom which he did not dispel. No young man filled with honorable ambition can encounter a difficulty which he did not meet and surmount. For centuries to come great men will trace their rise from humble origins to the inspirations of that lad who learned to read by the light of a pine-knot in a log-cabin; who, ragged and barefooted, trudged along the tow-path of the canal, and without money or affluent relations, without friends or assistance, by faith in himself and in God, became the most scholarly and best equipped statesman of his time, one of the foremost soldiers of his country, the best debater in the strongest of deliberative bodies, the leader of his party, and the Chief Magistrate of fifty millions of people before he was fifty years of age.

We are not here to question the ways of Providence. Our prayers were not answered as we desired, though the volume and fervor of our importunity seemed resistless; but already, behind the partially lifted veil, we see the fruits of the sacrifice. Old wounds are healed and fierce feuds forgotten. Vengeance and passion which have survived the best statesmanship of twenty years are dispelled by a common sorrow. Love follows sympathy.

Over this open grave the cypress and willow are indissolubly united, and into it are buried all sectional differences and hatreds. The North and the South rise from bended knees to embrace in the brotherhood of a common people and reunited country. Not this alone, but the humanity of the civilized world has been quickened and elevated, and the English-speaking people are nearer to-day in peace and unity than ever before. There is no language in which petitions have not arisen for Garfield's life, and no clime where tears have not fallen for his death. The Queen of the proudest of nations, for the first time in our recollections, brushes aside the formalities of diplomacy, and, descending from the throne, speaks for her own and the hearts of all her people, in the cable, to the afflicted wife, which says: "Myself and my children mourn with you."

It was my privilege to talk for hours with Gen. Garfield during his famous trip to the New York conference in the late canvass, and yet it was not conversation or discussion. He fastened upon me all the powers of inquisitiveness and acquisitiveness, and absorbed all I had learned in twenty years of the politics of this State. Under this restless and resistless craving for information, he drew upon all the resources of the libraries, gathered all the contents of the newspapers, and sought and sounded the opinions of all around him, and in his broad, clear mind the vast mass was so assimilated and tested that when he spoke or acted, it was accepted as true and wise. And yet it was by the gush and warmth of old college-chum ways, and not by the arts of the inquisitor, that when he had gained he never lost a friend. His strength was in ascertaining and expressing the average sense of his audience. I saw him at the Chicago Convention, and whenever that popular assemblage seemed drifting into hopeless confusion, his tall form commanded attention, and his clear voice and clear utterances instantly gave the accepted solution.

I arrived at his house at Mentor in the early morning following the disaster in Maine. While all about him were in panic, he saw only a damage which must and could be repaired. "It is no use bemoaning the past," he said; "the past has no uses except for its lessons." Business disposed of, he threw aside all restraint, and for hours his speculations and theories upon philosophy, government, education, eloquence; his criticism of books, his reminiscences of men and events, made that one of the white-letter days of my life. At Chickamauga he won his major-general's commission. On the anniversary of the battle he died. I shall never forget his description of the fight—so modest, yet graphic. It is imprinted on my memory as the most glorious battle-picture words ever painted. He thought the greatest calamity which could befall a man was to lose ambition. I said to him, "General, did you never in your earlier struggle have that feeling I have so often met with, when you would have compromised your future for a certainty, and if so, what?"

"Yes," said he, "I remember well when I would have been willing to exchange all the possibilities of my life for the certainty of a position as a successful teacher." Though he died neither a school principal nor college professor, and they seem humble achievements compared with what he did, his memory will instruct while time endures.

His long and dreadful sickness lifted the roof from his house and family circle, and his relations as son, husband, and father stood revealed in the broadest sunlight of publicity. The picture endeared him wherever is understood the full significance of that matchless word "Home." When he stood by the capitol just pronounced the President of the greatest and most powerful of republics, the exultation of the hour found its expression in a kiss upon the lips of his mother. For weeks, in distant Ohio, she sat by the gate watching for the hurrying feet of the messenger bearing the telegrams of hope or despair. His last conscious act was to write a letter of cheer and encouragement to that mother, and when the blow fell she illustrated the spirit she had instilled in him. There were no rebellious murmurings against the Divine dispensation, only in utter agony: "I have no wish to live longer; I will join him soon; the Lord's will be done." When Dr.

Bliss told him he had a bare chance of recovery, "Then," said he, "we will take that chance, doctor." When asked if he suffered pain, he answered: "If you can imagine a trip-hammer crashing on your body, or cramps such as you have in the water a thousand times intensified, you can have some idea of what I suffer." And yet, during those eighty-one days was heard neither groan nor complaint. Always brave and cheerful, he answered the fear of the surgeons with the remark: "I have faced death before; I am not afraid to meet him now." And again, "I have strength enough left to fight him yet"—and he could whisper to the Secretary of the Treasury an inquiry about the success of the funding scheme, and ask the Postmaster-General how much public money he had saved.

As he lay in the cottage by the sea, looking out upon the ocean, whose broad expanse was in harmony with his own grand nature, and heard the beating of the waves upon the shore, and felt the pulsations of millions of hearts against his chamber door, there was no posing for history and no preparation of last words for dramatic effect. With simple naturalness he gave the military salute to the sentinel gazing at his window, and that soldier, returning it in tears, will probably carry its memory to his dying day and transmit it to his children. The voice of his faithful wife came from her devotions in another room, singing, "Guide me, O Thou Great Jehovah."

"Listen," he cries, "is not that glorious?" and in a few hours heaven's portals opened and upborne upon prayers as never before wafted spirit above he entered the presence of God. It is the alleviation of all sorrow, public or private, that close upon it press the duties of and to the living.

The tolling bells, the minute-guns upon land and sea, the muffled drums and funeral hymns fill the air while our chief is borne to his last resting-place. The busy world is stilled for the hour when loving hands are preparing his grave. A stately shaft will rise, overlooking the lake and commemorating his deeds. But his fame will not live alone in marble or brass. His story will be treasured and kept warm in the hearts of millions for generations to come, and boys hearing it from their mothers will be fired with nobler ambitions. To his countrymen he will always be a typical American, soldier, and statesman. A year ago and not a thousand people of the old world had ever heard his name, and now there is scarcely a thousand who do not mourn his loss. The peasant loves him because from the same humble lot he became one of the mighty of earth, and sovereigns respect him because in his royal gifts and kingly nature God made him their equal.

CHAPTER XXXVI.
THE LESSONS OF HIS LIFE.

Probably the nearest and closest friend of

Garfield, intellectually speaking, was his successor in the presidency of Hiram College, B.A. Hinsdale. If any one understood the dead President
it was he. For many years they corresponded
regularly, exchanging views upon all topics that
interested either. They would not always agree,
but this necessarily followed from the mental independence of each. To Mr. Hinsdale we turn for
a trustworthy analysis of the character and intellectual greatness of his friend, and this he gives
us in an article published in the N.Y. *Independent*
of Sept. 29, 1881:

First of all, James A. Garfield had greatness
of nature. Were I limited to one sentence of
description, it would be: He was a great-natured man. He was a man of strong and massive body. A strong frame, broad shoulders,
powerful vital apparatus, and a massive head
furnished the physical basis of his life. He was
capable of an indefinite amount of work, both
physical and mental. His intellectual status
was equally strong and massive. He excelled
almost all men both in the patient accumu-
lation of facts and in bold generalization. He
had great power of logical analysis, and stood
with the first in rhetorical exposition. He had
the best instincts and habits of the scholar.
He loved to roam in every field of knowledge.
He delighted in the creations of the imagination—poetry, fiction, and art. He loved the
deep things of philosophy. He took a keen interest in scientific research. He gathered into

his storehouse the facts of history and politics, and threw over the whole the life and power of his own originality.

The vast labors that he crowded into those thirty years—labors rarely equaled in the history of men—are the fittest gauge of his physical and intellectual power. His moral character was on a scale equally large and generous. His feelings were delicate, his sympathies most responsive, his sense of justice keen. He was alive to delicate points of honor. No other man whom I have known had such heart. He had great faith in human nature and was wholly free from jealousy and suspicion. He was one of the most helpful and appreciative of men. His largeness of views and generosity of spirit were such that he seemed incapable of personal resentment. He was once exhorted to visit moral indignation upon some men who had wronged him deeply. Fully appreciating the baseness of their conduct, he said he would try, but added: 'I am afraid some one will have to help me.'

What is more, General Garfield was religious, both by nature and by habit. His mind was strong in the religious element. His near relatives received the Gospel as it was proclaimed fifty years ago by Thomas and Alexander Campbell. He made public profession of religion before he reached his twentieth year and became a member of the same church, and such he remained until his death. Like all men of his thought and reading, he understood the

hard questions that modern science and criticism have brought into the field of religion.
Whether he ever wrought these out to his
own full satisfaction I can not say. However
that may be, his native piety, his early training, and his sober convictions held him fast to
the great truths of revealed religion. Withal,
he was a man of great simplicity of character.
No one could be more approachable. He drew
men to him as the magnet the iron filings. This
he did naturally and without conscious plan or
effort. At times, when the burden of work was
heavy and his strength overdrawn, intimate
friends would urge him to withdraw himself
somewhat from the crowds that flocked to
him; but almost always the advice was vain.
His sympathy with the people was immediate
and quick. He seemed almost intuitively to
read the public thought and feeling. No matter what was his station, he always remembered the rock from which he had himself
been hewn. Naturally he inspired confidence
in all men who came into contact with him.
When a young man, and even a boy, he ranked
in judgment and in counsel with those much
his seniors.

It is not remarkable, therefore, that he
should have led a great career. He was always with the foremost or in the lead, no
matter what the work in hand. He was a good
wood-chopper and a good canal hand; he was
a good school janitor; and, upon the whole,
ranked all competitors, both in Hiram and in

Williamstown, as a student. He was an excellent teacher. He was the youngest man in the Ohio Senate. When made brigadier-general, he was the youngest man of that rank in the army. When he entered it, he was the youngest man on the floor of the House of Representatives. His great ability and signal usefulness as teacher, legislator, popular orator, and President must be passed with a single reference.

He retained his simplicity and purity of character to the end. Neither place nor power corrupted his honest fiber. Advancement in public favor and position gave him pleasure, but brought him no feeling of elation. For many years President Garfield and the writer exchanged letters at the opening of each new year. January 5th, last, he wrote:

"For myself, the year has been full of surprises, and has brought more sadness than joy. I am conscious of two things: first, that I have never had, and do not think I shall take, the Presidential fever. Second, that I am not elated with the election to that office. On the contrary, while appreciating the honor and the opportunities which the place brings, I feel heavily the loss of liberty which accompanies it, and especially that it will in a great measure stop my growth."

March 26, 1881, in the midst of the political tempest following his inauguration, he wrote: "I throw you a line across the storm, to let you know that I think, when I have a moment between breaths, of the dear old quiet and peace of Hiram and Mentor." How he longed for "the dear old quiet and peace of Hiram and Mentor" in the weary days following the assassin's shot all readers of the newspapers know already.

Such are some main lines in the character of this great-natured and richly-cultured man. The outline is but poor and meager. Well do I remember the days following the Chicago Convention, when the biographers flocked to Mentor. How hard they found it to compress within the limits both of their time and their pages the life, services, and character of their great subject. One of these discouraged historians one day wearily said: "General, how much there is of you!"

Space fails to speak of President Garfield's short administration. Fortunately, it is not necessary. Nor can I give the history of the assassination or sketch the gallant fight for life. His courage and fortitude, faith and hope, patience and tenderness are a part of his country's history. Dying, as well as living, he maintained his great position with appropriate power and dignity. His waving his white hand to the inmates of the White House, the morning he was borne sick out of it, reminds one of dying Sidney's motioning the cup of water to the lips of the wounded soldier. No man's life was ever prayed for by so many people. The name of no living man has been upon so many lips. No sick-bed was ever the subject of so much tender solicitude. That one so strong in faculties, so rich in knowledge, so ripe in experience, so noble in character, so needful to the nation, and so dear to his friends should be taken in a way so foul almost taxes faith in the Divine love and wisdom. Perhaps, however, in the noble lessons of those eighty days from July 2d to September 19th, and in the moral unification of the country, history will find full compensation for our great loss.

Finally, the little white-haired mother and the constant wife must not be passed unnoticed. How the old mother prayed and waited, and the brave wife wrought and hoped, will live forever, both in history and in legend. It is not impiety to say that wheresoever President Garfield's story shall be told in the whole world there shall also this, that these women have done, be told for a memorial of them.

THE END.

APPENDIX
TRUE OR FALSE?

This book includes the following statements. Do you agree with them?

Success comes to him who is in earnest (page 24).

Seek all knowledge, however trifling, and there will come a time when you can make use of it (page 48).

Every man ought to feel an honorable ambition to succeed as well as possible in his chosen path (page 50).

Generally work comes to him who earnestly seeks it (page 62).

We never fully know anything till we have tried to impart it to others (page 85).

No work is humiliating which is undertaken with a right aim and a useful object (page 93).

I doubt whether any man of great powers can permanently bury himself, no matter how obscure the position which he chooses. Sooner or later the world will find him out, and he will be lifted to his rightful place (page 123).

Poverty is very inconvenient, but it is a fine spur to activity, and may be made a rich blessing (page 124).

Greatness has its penalties, and a low estate its compensations (page 126).

Whatever is worth doing at all is worth doing well (pages 140–41).

Northeast Ohio exceeds any other portion of the State in its devotion to the cause of education and the general intelligence of its inhabitants (page 173).

A man who is destined to be great is only strengthened by opposition, and rises in the end victorious over circumstances (page 185).

Truly great men do not seem to realize their greatness (page 209).

The kind heart and the open hand never accompany a suspicious, distrustful mind. Designing men mark such a character for their own selfishness (page 214).

Garfield's life constitutes an example for the American youth, which will never be lost nor grow dim (page 214).

On Garfield: No character in American history furnishes a brighter or more inspiring example to boys and young men (page 237).

No boy in poverty almost hopeless, thirsting for knowledge, meets an obstacle which Garfield did not experience and overcome. No youth despairing in darkness feels a gloom which he did not dispel. No young man filled with honorable ambition can encounter a difficulty which he did not meet and surmount (page 238).

Love follows sympathy (page 239).

It is no use bemoaning the past; the past has no uses except for its lessons (page 240).

VOCABULARY

The meaning of words changes over time. So does their usage. For example, *From Canal Boy to President* emphasizes how James A. Garfield was *earnest*. Today he might be described as *having a passion* for his various jobs and duties. What did it mean to be *in earnest*? Study of the meaning of key words, as they were recorded in the dictionaries of the period, can lead to better understanding and valuable insight.

The words below are often used, or used in important places, throughout the biography. In many cases the twenty-first-century meaning of the word appears alongside other usages that have fallen away. We no longer think of our *character*, for example, as something like our handwriting (or *penmanship*, as this is called in the book).

Definitions for the following words are taken from Noah Webster's *American Dictionary of the English Language*, which was the standard for American dictionaries when *From Canal Boy to President* was first published.

AWKWARD, adjective. 1. Wanting dexterity in the use of the hands or of instruments; unready; not dexterous; bungling; untoward. 2. Inelegant; unpolite; ungraceful in manners; clumsy; unnatural; bad.

CHARACTER, noun. 1. A mark made by cutting or engraving, as on stone, metal or other hard material; hence, a mark or figure made with a pen or style, on paper, or other material used to contain writing; a letter, or figure used to form words, and communicate ideas....3. The manner of writing; the peculiar from of letters used by a particular person. 4. The peculiar qualities, impressed by nature or habit on a person, which distinguish him from others; these constitute real character, and the qualities which he is supposed to possess, constitute his estimated character, or reputation. Hence we say, a character is not formed, when the person has not acquired stable and distinctive qualities.

COURAGE, noun. Bravery; intrepidity; that quality of mind which enables men to encounter danger and difficulties with firmness, or without fear or depression of spirits; valor; boldness; resolution. It is a constituent part of fortitude; but fortitude implies patience to bear continued suffering.

DIGNITY, noun. 1. True honor; nobleness or elevation of mind, consisting in a high sense of propriety, truth and justice, with an abhorrence of mean and sinful actions; opposed to meanness. In this sense, we speak of the dignity of mind, and dignity of sentiments. This dignity is based on moral rectitude; all vice is incompatible with true dignity of mind. The man who deliberately injures another, whether male or female, has no true dignity of soul. 2. Elevation; honorable place or rank of elevation; degree of excellence, either in estimation, or in the order of nature. Man is superior in dignity to brutes.

DUTY, noun. 1. That which a person owes to another; that which a person is bound, by any natural, moral or legal obligation, to pay, do or perform. Obedience to princes, magistrates and the laws is the *duty* of every citizen and subject; obedience, respect and kindness to parents are *duties* of children; fidelity to friends is a *duty*; reverence, obedience and prayer to God are indispensable *duties*; the government and religious instruction of children are *duties* of parents which they cannot neglect without guilt.

EARNEST, adjective. 1. Ardent in the pursuit of an object; eager to obtain; having a longing desire; warmly engaged or incited. 2. Ardent; warm; eager; zealous; animated; importunate; as *earnest in love; earnest in prayer.* 3. Intent; fixed. 4. Serious; important; that is, really intent or engaged; whence the phrase, *in earnest.* To be *in earnest* is to be really urging or stretching towards an object; intent on a pursuit.

FIRMNESS, noun. 1. Closeness or denseness of texture or structure; compactness; hardness; solidity; as the *firmness* of wood, stone, cloth or other substance. 2. Stability; strength; as the *firmness* of a union, or of a confederacy. 3. Steadfastness; constancy; fixedness; as the *firmness* of a purpose or resolution; the *firmness* of a man, or of his courage; *firmness* of mind or soul.

GENEROUS, adjective. 1. Primarily, being of honorable birth or origin; hence, noble; honorable; magnanimous; applied to persons; as *a generous foe; a generous critic.* 2. Noble; honorable; applied to things; as *a generous virtue; generous boldness.* It is used also to denote like qualities in irrational animals; as *a generous pack of hounds.*

3. Liberal; bountiful; munificent; free to give; as *a generous friend; a generous father*. 4. Strong; full of spirit; as *generous wine*. 5. Full; overflowing; abundant; as *a generous cup; a generous table*. 6. Sprightly; courageous; as *a generous steed*.

GREAT, adjective. 1. Large in bulk or dimensions; a term of comparison, denoting more magnitude or extension than something else, or beyond what is usual; as *a great house; a great farm*. 2. Being of extended length or breadth; as *a great distance; a great lake*. 3. Large in number; as *a great many*. 4. Expressing a large, extensive or unusual degree of any thing; as *great fear; great love; great strength; great wealth; great power; great influence; great folly*. 5. Long continued; as *a great while*. 6. Important; weighty; as *a great argument; a great truth; a great event; a thing of no great consequence; it is no great matter*. 7. Chief; principal; as *the great seal of England*. 8. Chief; of vast power and excellence; supreme; illustrious; *as the great God; the great Creator*. 9. Vast; extensive; wonderful; admirable. 10. Possessing large or strong powers of mind; as *a great genius*. 11. Having made extensive or unusual acquisitions of science or knowledge; as *a great philosopher or botanist; a great scholar*. 12. Distinguished by rank, office or power; elevated; eminent; as *a great lord; the great men of the nation; the great Mogul; Alexander the great*. 13. Dignified in aspect, mien or manner. 14. Magnanimous; generous; of elevated sentiments; high-minded. He has *a great soul*. 15. Rich; sumptuous; magnificent. *A great feast or entertainment*. 16. Vast; sublime; as *a great con-*

ception or idea. 17. Dignified; noble. 18. Swelling; proud; as, *he was not disheartened by great looks.* 19. Chief; principal; much traveled; as *a great road.* The ocean is called *the great highway of nations.* 20. Pregnant; teeming; as *great with young.* 21. Hard; difficult. *It is no great matter to live in peace with meek people.* 22. Familiar; intimate. [*Vulgar.*] 23. Distinguished by extraordinary events, or unusual importance. 24. Denoting a degree of consanguinity, in the ascending or descending line, as *great grandfather, the father of a grandfather; great great grandfather, the father of a great grandfather, and so on indefinitely; and great grandson, great great grandson. etc.* 25. Superior; preeminent; as *great chamberlain; great marshal.*

HABIT, noun....1. Garb; dress; clothes in general...4. A disposition or condition of the mind or body acquired by custom or a frequent repetition of the same act. *Habit* is that which is held or retained, the effect of custom or frequent repetition. Hence we speak of good habits and bad habits. Frequent drinking of spirits leads to a habit of intemperance. We should endeavor to correct evil habits by a change of practice. A great point in the education of children, is to prevent the formation of bad habits.

HUMBLE, adjective. 1. Low; opposed to high or lofty. 2. Low; opposed to lofty or great; mean; not magnificent; as *a humble cottage.* 3. Lowly; modest; meek; submissive; opposed to proud, haughty, arrogant or assuming.

INDUSTRY, noun. Habitual diligence in any employment, either bodily or mental; steady attention to business; assiduity; opposed to sloth and idleness. We are directed to take lessons of industry from the bee. *Industry pays debts, while idleness or despair will increase them.*

INTEGRITY, noun. 1. Wholeness; entireness; unbroken state. The constitution of the United States guaranties to each state the *integrity* of its territories. The contracting parties guarantied the *integrity* of the empire. 2. The entire, unimpaired state of any thing, particularly of the mind; moral soundness or purity; incorruptness; uprightness; honesty. *Integrity* comprehends the whole moral character, but has a special reference to uprightness in mutual dealings, transfers of property, and agencies for others. The moral grandeur of *independent integrity* is the sublimest thing in nature, before which the pomp of eastern magnificence and the splendor of conquest are odious as well as perishable. 3. Purity; genuine, unadulterated, unimpaired state; as *the integrity of language.*

KNOWLEDGE, noun. 1. A clear and certain perception of that which exists, or of truth and fact; the perception of the connection and agreement, or disagreement and repugnancy of our ideas. 2. Learning; illumination of mind. *Ignorance is the curse of God, knowledge the wing wherewith we fly to heaven.* 3. Skill; as *a knowledge of seamanship.* 4. Acquaintance with any fact or person. *I have no knowledge of the man or thing.* 5. Cognizance; notice. 6. Information; power of knowing.

LIBERAL, adjective. 1. Of a free heart; free to give or bestow; not close or contracted; munificent; bountiful; generous; giving largely; as a *liberal* donor; the *liberal* founders of a college or hospital. It expresses less than profuse or extravagant. 2. Generous; ample; large; as *a liberal donation; a liberal allowance.* 3. Not selfish, narrow on contracted; catholic; enlarged; embracing other interests than one's own; as *liberal* sentiments or views; a *liberal mind; liberal policy.* 4. General; extensive; embracing literature and the sciences generally; as *a liberal education.* This phrase is often but not necessarily synonymous with collegiate; as a collegiate education. 5. Free; open; candid; as a *liberal* communication of thoughts.

NOBILITY, noun. 1. Dignity of mind; greatness; grandeur; that elevation of soul which comprehends bravery, generosity, magnamimity, intrepidity, and contempt of every thing that dishonors character. 2. Antiquity of family; descent from noble ancestors; distinction by blood, usually joined with riches. 3. The qualities which constitute distinction of rank in civil society, according to the customs or laws of the country; that eminence or dignity which a man derives from birth or title conferred, and which places him in an order above common men.

PERSEVERANCE, noun. 1. Persistence in any thing undertaken; continued pursuit or prosecution of any business or enterprise begun; applied alike to good or evil.

POLITICAL, adjective. Pertaining to policy, or to civil government and its administration. *Political* measures or affairs are measures that respect the government of a nation or state. So we say, *political power* or *authority; political wisdom; a political scheme; political opinions.* A good prince is the *political* father of his people. The founders of a state and wise senators are also called *political* fathers.

PROVIDENCE, noun. 1. The act of providing or preparing for future use or application. 2. Foresight; timely care; particularly, active foresight, or foresight accompanied with the procurement of what is necessary for future use, or with suitable preparation. *How many of the troubles and perplexities of life proceed from want of providence!* 3. In theology, the care and superintendence which God exercises over his creatures.... A belief in divine *providence* is a source of great consolation to good men. By divine *providence* is often understood God himself.

PUBLIC, adjective. 1. Pertaining to a nation, state or community; extending to a whole people; as *a public law,* which binds the people of a nation or state, as opposed to a *private statute* or *resolve,* which respects an individual or a corporation only. Thus we say, *public welfare, public good, public calamity, public service, public property.* 2. Common to many; current or circulated among people of all classes; general; as *public report; public scandal.* 3. Open; notorious; exposed to all persons without restriction. 4. Regarding the community; directed to the interest of a nation, state or community; as *public spirit; public mindedness*; opposed to *private* or *selfish.* 5. Open for general entertainment; as *a public house.* 6. Open to common use; as *a public road.* 7. In general, *public* expresses something common to mankind at large, to a nation, state, city or town, and is opposed to *private*, which denotes what belongs to an individual, to a family, to a company or corporation.

RESOLVE, noun. 1. Fixed purpose of mind; settled determination; resolution.

SCHOLAR, noun. 1. One who learns of a teacher; one who is under the tuition of a preceptor; a pupil; a disciple; hence, any member of a college, academy or school; applicable to the learner of any art, science or branch of literature. 2. A man of letters. 3. Emphatically used, a man eminent for erudition; a person of high attainments in science or literature.

SERVICE, noun. 1. In a general sense, labor of body or of body and mind, performed at the command of a superior, or the pursuance of duty, or for the benefit of another. Service is voluntary or involuntary. Voluntary service is that of hired servants, or of contract, or of persons who spontaneously perform something for another's benefit. Involuntary service is that of slaves, who work by compulsion....8. Actual duty; that which is required to be done in an office; as, to perform the services of a clerk, a sherif or judge.

SYMPATHY, noun. 1. Fellow feeling; the quality of being affected by the affection of another, with feelings by the affection of another, with feelings correspondent in kind, if not in degree. We feel sympathy for another when we see him in distress, or when we are informed of his distresses. This sympathy is a correspondent feeling of pain or regret. 2. An agreement of affections or inclinations, or a conformity of natural temperament, which makes two persons pleased with each other.

VOCATION, noun. 1. Among divines, a calling by the will of God; or the bestowment of God's distinguishing grace upon a person or nation, by which that person or nation is put in the way of salvation; as *the vocation of the Jews under the old dispensation, and of the Gentiles under the gospel.* 2. Summons; call; inducement. 3. Designation or destination to a particular state or profession. 4. Employment; calling; occupation; trade; a word that includes professions as well as mechanical occupations.